MARKETING MESS

TO

BRAND SUCCESS

MARKETING MESS

TO
BRAND SUCCESS

30 Challenges to Transform Your Organization's Brand (and Your Own)

SCOTT JEFFREY MILLER

Wall Street Journal bestselling author and former Chief Marketing Officer, FranklinCovey Co.

mango
PUBLISHING

CORAL GABLES

For permission requests, please contact the publisher at:
Mango Publishing Group
2850 S Douglas Road, 2nd Floor
Coral Gables, FL 33134 USA
info@mangopublishinggroup.com

For special orders, quantity sales, course adoptions, and corporate sales, please email the publisher at sales@mango.bz. For trade and wholesale sales, please contact Ingram Publisher Services at customer.service@ingramcontent.com or +1.800.509.4887.

Marketing Mess to Brand Success: 30 Challenges to Transform Your Organization's Brand (and Your Own)

ISBN:(p) 978-1-64250-380-7 (e) 978-1-64250-381-4

Library of Congress Control Number: pending

BISAC category code: BUS019000, BUSINESS & ECONOMICS / Decision-Making & Problem Solving

Printed in the United States of America

TABLE OF CONTENTS

INTRODUCTION

When I first wrote *Management Mess to Leadership Success,* I had no idea how it would be received or how it would change my own life. The idea started out simply enough—there were over 100,000 leadership books available on Amazon, replete with academic musings, principle-laden insights, inspirational stories (told by a diverse field ranging from CEOs to former Navy Seals), and new ways of understanding and harnessing the human psyche. There are many gems to be found among these books and I spend a good deal of my time interviewing and learning from their authors. I truly love and treasure many of these titles, but they were not the kind of book I wanted to write.

In taking stock of my own journey, I felt a strong pull toward being completely open and honest—to some, maybe too much so. That meant acknowledging and unpacking many of my career missteps, bad assumptions, or outright failures. I hadn't crystalized this desire into the theme of "messes" yet; I just felt I couldn't authentically share my experiences with a highlight reel of just my home runs. To authentically convey my journey, I needed many of the foul balls and forced errors highlighted as well. Why? Because on reflection, that's where I often learned the most, grew the most, or developed a sensitivity to better spot both messes and successes down the road. It was with this insight that the charge of "Own your mess" began to take shape. But even then, I had no idea how much this concept would resonate with others.

I'm fortunate to be a guest on a number of podcasts and to present as a keynote speaker at both public and private events. Almost without fail, what I am asked about most is my willingness to be so open and vulnerable in making it safe for very competent professionals to acknowledge and "own" their messes. If I was unsure if I had tapped into something real and pressing in people's lives, that was put to rest in a speech to nearly seven thousand conference attendees at Rachel Hollis's RISE Business event in Charleston, South Carolina. This massive audience closed my speech by chanting, "Own your mess," in unison over and over again. It was incredibly validating. We all have messes to face up to, and if we shirk that experience and fail to learn from them, our careers, our relationships, and even our sense of who we truly are will be compromised. And perhaps more importantly, when leaders own their messes, they make it safe for others to own theirs. And that's a culture everyone wants to engage in.

On the flip side, as I now author the second book in the *Mess to Success* series—focused on marketing— one might be tempted to wonder: *Just how many messes did you make, Scott?* Or to continue with my baseball analogy, am I setting myself up as the professional equivalent of the Bad News Bears? My short answer is not only no, but hell no. Messes are the byproduct of *doing*. Famed fiction author Neil Gaiman said it perfectly: "[I]f you are making mistakes, then you are making new things, trying new things, learning, living, pushing yourself, changing yourself, changing your world. You are doing things you have never done before, and more importantly, you are Doing Something." So go ahead and own your messes, because they are the by-product of you in motion—living, growing, taking risks, setting goals, stepping outside your comfort zone, and making a mark in the world. Conversely, the only formula for avoiding messes is to do nothing. So yes, I'll take my messes, thank you very much. And that includes my marketing messes.

While I served as the chief marketing officer for a large, multinational public company, an associate once announced that I "knew *nothing* about marketing." And this was someone I had specifically recruited and hired after lobbying to fund their new role! And in case you were wondering, the rebuke didn't come during a private conversation over drinks. They proclaimed it in front of four of the organization's directors—all of whom reported to me as well.

You know nothing, Scott Miller.

If you're not a *Game of Thrones* fan, just ignore that last part and keep reading.

How many marketing messes does it take to earn such a critique? More than one, I'm sure. Probably a lot. So for this book, I've selected thirty of the most common marketing messes (and potential successes) that professionals will face throughout their career—whatever the level of your role, size of your organization, or focus of your industry. Not all of them are my messes; I've made my share of mistakes over three decades of formal and informal marketing roles, and I've also seen a bevy of them from others. Many of the messes in this book are either drawn from my own experiences or those I've witnessed and been dragged into in some way or another. As such, you may find that this book serves as a kind of marketing career guide as well, and that's fine. What this book *isn't* is a manual on the "four Ps" of marketing (product, price, placement, and promotion) or what to do on Day One of your new marketing role. If you're looking for that level of instruction, you're not only reading the wrong book, you've probably said yes to the wrong job. However, if you want to purchase the book and use the jacket to hide your *Fifty Shades* novel on the flight home or *The Subtle Art of Not Giving a F*ck* on the way to your performance review, please feel free.

Moving from the topic of management in the first *Mess to Success* book to marketing came inadvertently from one of my coaches. She told me that I was always in persuasion mode—always trying to convince and influence people to think like me, follow my lead, believe what I believe, or do what I want them to do. Ironically, she meant it as a critique of my style and personality, but I took it as a compliment (despite the eye roll when I thanked her). But it got me thinking that persuasion—convincing someone or some group to understand what you believe to be true— is really what marketing is all about. Ideally, this translates into that individual or group adopting your service, hiring your brand, contributing to your cause, voting for your candidate, or buying your product. It's great when they do, and it is your fault when they don't. Welcome to marketing.

In my role as chief marketing officer at FranklinCovey, I took part in many global launches. This included running focus groups; administering alphas and betas; conducting quality tests; designing new logos; writing taglines; approving fonts; engaging in advertising campaigns; creating press releases; producing radio, print, and digital ads; hosting live events; and more. I've had my hand in slide decks; workbooks; giveaways and tchotchkes; email campaigns; websites; banner ads; pay-per-clicks; sponsorships; SEO; marketing automation; direct mail; press proofs; trade shows (lots of trade shows); webcasts; podcasts; print, digital, and audio books of every conceivable length and format; magazine columns; conference keynotes; satellite downlinks; live broadcast events for global audiences; and... You get the idea. The list is endless. I've written more text than most Madison Avenue writers and proofed more catalogs and newsletters than many seasoned editors. If you're one to measure all that marketing scar tissue in hours, I've more than hit the "expert" 10,000-hours mark. More like ten times that! All of which is not to brag about how wonderful and experienced I am as a marketer, but to convince you I've done my time with my sleeves rolled up in the trenches. You could spend the same number of hours in your own marketing trenches and walk away with similar insights and instincts, or you could get a head start by reading this book. Personally, I'd recommend the latter.

Based on the impact of the first book in the *Mess to Success* series— *Management Mess to Leadership Success: 30 Challenges to Become the Leader You Would Follow*—this volume follows a similar pattern: there are thirty challenges, organized so that you can read the themes most relevant to you at any given moment, or in order from one to thirty. The thirty challenges can be incorporated into your monthly calendar (one a day if you're feeling up to it) and implemented by following the "Mess to Success" prompts at the end of each challenge. This is a book that is designed to be yours, so dog-ear the pages, underline passages, read it in bite-size chunks or all at once, and even photocopy it for colleagues— wait, don't do that. Everything else though, go for it.

As I alluded to earlier, the marketing challenges I'm offering in this book are to not only acknowledge your messes but to *own* them. That means to study them, reflect on them, tease out principles from them, ultimately learn from them and, perhaps most importantly, freely share them with others. Because just as you learn from your own messes, the true gift of leadership is allowing others to also learn from your messes. And when I say, "learn," I'm talking about the kind of insight that changes not only how you move forward, but how quickly you can see what's ahead. Think of it like that old TV gameshow *Name That Tune*. The challenge for the players was to earn points by responding to a musical clue and announcing how many notes it would take to identify a particular song. Each player would bid against the other, driving the number of notes down until one player finally passed and declared, "Okay then, name that tune!" And therefore, the opponent often had to identify the song in a second or two.

How many marketing notes does it take for you to name your mess? If you step up to the challenge of owning yours and learning from mine, you'll see and identify them long before the music (i.e., your marketing career) is over.

CHALLENGE 1

IT'S THE CUSTOMER, STUPID

Have you become so distracted by your internal focus,
that you've lost external focus on your customers?

A popular adage is "Those who do not learn history are doomed to repeat it." So here's a short lesson in history to start us off.

One of the greatest political campaigns of our lifetime was the 1992 United States presidential election. For the first time in recent history, there were three viable candidates in the general election. Three, you ask? Yep, Ross Perot made a surprisingly strong independent bid and (many say) tipped the election away from President George H. W. Bush to then Governor Bill Clinton hailing from, of all places, Arkansas (not exactly a proven launching pad for the presidency). It was likely headed that way regardless of Perot, but his role in challenging the traditional two-party system paved the way for the Reform Party (which didn't last) and then gave rise to the Tea Party Republicans, who to this day have forever changed the face of the Grand Old Party. For good or bad remains to be seen.

At the time, President Bush (later known as "Bush 41" because of his son's future ascent to that office) was coming off an unprecedented 90 percent presidential approval rating after the first Gulf War, precipitated by the Iraqi invasion of Kuwait. Many thought there was no possible way he could lose reelection. But, as we know, political highs are fleeting, and the U.S. economy was headed south with a 7.4 percent unemployment rate,[1] and the U.S. savings and loan meltdown was wiping out hundreds of banks and decimating entire communities across America. The Clinton/ Gore campaign was the first time in modern history where the Democratic ticket featured two Southerners (Bill Clinton was the governor of Arkansas and Al Gore was a U.S. senator from Tennessee), and fairly young ones at that.

In the midst of all the rumored Clinton… let's call them "dalliances," one of the Democrats' secret weapons was a duo named James Carville and Paul Begala, two new political operatives who went on to achieve global fame as pundits, authors, speakers, and strategists. One of my

---

1   Amadeo, Kimberly, (2019) "Unemployment Rate by Year Since 1929 Compared to Inflation and GDP." *The Balance*, 14 Dec., Available from: https://www.thebalance.com/unemployment-rate-by-year-3305506.

favorite books ever written is by James and Paul, titled *Buck Up, Suck Up…* *and Come Back When You Foul Up.*

These two are widely credited with winning the 1992 election for Clinton and Gore by establishing the first modern political "war room" that served as a communications hub and supported a rapid-response messaging strategy that generated the now-famed phrase "It's the Economy, Stupid." (What the sign in the room actually said was "The Economy, Stupid," but it morphed into "*It's* the Economy, Stupid," so for the purpose of this chapter, we'll go with that.) This was a reference to that fact that the likely way they were going to beat this otherwise very popular incumbent president was to stay insanely focused in their messaging and pound hard on the failing economy. To this day, I can envision the sign in the Clinton Little Rock campaign headquarters that became iconic for decades: "*It's the Economy, Stupid.*"

The rest is history, and President Bush served one term, not to be confused with his son George W. Bush "43," who served two.

I share this political story because "It's the Economy, Stupid" is to political campaigns what "It's the Customer, Stupid" is to marketing teams.

Marketers need to take what they do as seriously as if we were trying to win the White House. After all, political strategists are, in their simplest forms, marketers—just much better paid.

And like any political campaign, in marketing it's so easy to get distracted. In elections, your opponent is always trying to lure you off message and move you away from your preferred talking points. Many of you may not recall this, but for much of the 1988 presidential campaign, Bush vs. Dukakis, the key issue (are you sitting down?) became flag burning. For months, this topic consumed the nation—was it your right to burn the American flag? I'm not kidding, this was the core issue across America for many months, and both major party candidates found themselves consumed talking about it at every campaign stop. We see it in every election—a polarizing issue is thrown out (or likely cooked up by one of the candidate's camps), then the other person campaigning for office is constantly forced to be on the defensive; or worse, stake out a hasty position they'd not put much thought into. Sadly, it still works well for distracting both the opposition candidate and the voting public.

In marketing, the same issue exists. However, it's typically not outside forces cooking up distractions; rather, they're created internally, and not just by the broader company but likely right inside the marketing division. It's not an indictment, it's simply human behavior. Focus is hard and becoming harder for everyone as we face increasingly unlimited options in life and work. A key leadership competency is the ability to focus on winnable priorities and limit tempting distractions every one of us is prone to pursue. Focus is also emerging as a key marketing competency in a world of limitless channels, platforms, customers, segments, metrics, messages, etc.

As I follow this chapter with twenty-nine more challenges, I want to remind you to center yourself and your marketing team on your customer. This may sound like a no-brainer, but it's likely one of the biggest ongoing temptations you will face. I'm not sure I truly ever did center on the customer, and it's likely one of my biggest marketing messes. I centered myself instead around the priorities of the C-suite and our own company needs. *Leading up* was a genius career strategy that ensured my tenure and influence, although some may call it *kissing up*. While I was no sycophant, I was very adept at ensuring the team I led executed internally identified priorities, many of which, in hindsight, were not always customer-focused. Many of us unwittingly fall into this same reality, regardless of our professional roles (marketing, finance, innovation, sales, operations, etc.), and I was no different. Take your judgment elsewhere; welcome to professional life for most of us. The instinct to survive and thrive internally, in any culture, frequently gravitates our efforts away from our clients' needs. This truism exists in the public and private sector, in for-profit and nonprofit companies, in government and the political arena—everywhere. The more you are aware of this natural human condition to focus internally on your organization (and thus your own relevance), the more you can redirect it outwardly toward your customer (and eventually increase your relevance exponentially).

Somewhat unique to marketing inside organizations is that everyone seems to have an opinion about your previous, current, and future campaigns. I can't ever recall sitting in a meeting where I offered finance advice on calculating EBITDA or shared my technical theories around cloud computing with IT. Perhaps I should have returned the unsolicited favor more often. If I had a dollar for every time I sat in an executive team meeting, turned to a different functional leader, and said, "You know, based on that genius comment, you should be in marketing." As a marketer, your main governing responsibility is to represent the customer and keep the focus tethered there. You will be tempted at every juncture to become distracted by internal forces and opinions. Resist. You're likely your own worst enemy when it comes to maintaining an obsessive focus on your customer by falling victim to perhaps well-intended but typically distracting and often contradictory internal perspectives. Make a sign like the one in the Clinton/Gore war room so everyone who comes into your office, division, building, campus, or virtual meeting is reminded that the lens through which you see everything is that of the customer: "*It's the Customer, Stupid.*" If you're so inclined, you could make it the image of your Zoom background.

It may fatigue others—hell, it may fatigue you—but it's the right thing to do. Not only does being customer-focused come with a better alignment of your marketing assets, it allows you to act as a conduit to other divisions who will, with good reason, likely never meet a customer. And if such divisions are talking to customers, it's likely to collect on a late invoice or solve a shipping issue. Your role in marketing is to get as close to the customer as possible so you can represent them in meetings and even articulate their needs better than they can—and do it in their own language. I'm reminded of this profound quote from Steve Jobs as it relates to your marketing connection with clients:

> *Some people say, "Give the customers what they want." But that's not my approach. Our job is to figure out what they're going to want before they do. I think Henry Ford once said, "If I'd asked customers what they wanted, they would have told me, 'A faster horse!'" People don't know what they want until you show it to them. That's why I*

never rely on market research. Our task is to read things that are not yet on the page.[2]

Fulfilling Steve's vision requires your becoming a bit of a futurist, balanced with extraordinary curiosity and listening skills. It takes some bravado, seasoned with patience and humility, to predict what your clients want before they even know it. Too much guessing will have you building solutions no one cares about. And too much complacency will leave you in the dust of your competition. Predicting customers' needs requires a somewhat unnatural focus on hearing their voice.

This customer obsession will require you to leave the office and miss key company "do not miss" meetings, which might jeopardize your internal political stature. Again, this mindset and practice is the right thing to do. Spend as much time with current and even prospective customers as is feasible so you're the sane voice back in the office about what's really going on out there. Could you "customer-focus" yourself out of a job? Possibly, depending on your company's culture; but ultimately, you must decide how to balance your time, budget, and attention. Much of marketing is, in fact, understanding the politics of your internal organization and thriving in the midst of it.

I spent a lot of time in the field during my tenure as a chief marketing officer, but as I look back, it was primarily with our sales teams. I listened to their needs, which were always legitimate "in the moment," and that drove much of what our marketing team developed in the form of support tools. On reflection, however, I was generally one step removed from the customer. Not always: I presented and facilitated hundreds of marketing events where clients attended; thus I "met" thousands of clients over the years. That was great for my corporate image, but I was also always doing 100 percent of the talking. Flying into Cleveland for a three-hour, company-hosted marketing event and presenting our value proposition to chief learning officers and human resources directors and shaking hands was a weekly occurrence. That was followed by jumping into a

---

2   Isaacson, Walter, *Steve Jobs*, New York: Simon & Schuster, 2015.

taxi, and repeating it again in Boston the next day. This was not being externally *customer*-focused, it was being internally *company*-focused. And I was superb at it. But if I had to do it over again, I would spend less time managing my brand inside the company and more time visiting and listening to real customers and their needs outside the company. I hope the thousands of clients I met and cared about never felt this from me; but if you're also brutally honest, you can see yourself in the same scenario. Sometimes doing your job is, in fact, not the real job you should be doing. Let that sink in and adapt it to your situation.

I want this first challenge to set a foundation to buffer you against the everyday temptation during your marketing career to be sucked into the hairball and instead help you learn to orbit it. I'm going to give you many book recommendations throughout this manuscript, so keep your credit card handy. One of my top ten recommendations is *Orbiting the Giant Hairball: A Corporate Fool's Guide to Surviving with Grace* by Gordon MacKenzie—a must-read for everyone in a marketing role. It's not focused on marketing per se, but it is a masterful tome on recognizing the hairball (that's your company) and how to avoid its deadly gravitational pull sucking you inward, thus distracting you from your customer.

It's the story of how Shoebox greeting cards, which is the avant-garde division of the otherwise more conservative Hallmark Cards, came into being. It's a masterpiece, and after you read it, you will never manage your marketing career the same. It's your job as a leader in marketing to become the voice of the customer. Other divisions in the company will naturally try to suck you away from the client and back into "knitting" the hairball. This doesn't mean they're evil, incompetent, or ignorant of the customer, it's just a fact that their role is typically different and perhaps naturally more inwardly focused. As a marketer, it requires a tremendous level of courage, discipline, focus, stamina, and diplomacy to resist this temptation at all costs. The "hairball" (your company) only exists because of the customer. So in the genius words of the internationally acclaimed and world-renowned author Scott Jeffrey Miller, "It's the Customer, Stupid."

FROM MESS TO SUCCESS:

IT'S THE CUSTOMER, STUPID

- Spend the next few days quietly listening in every meeting you attend and lead.

  - Monitor how many times your customer is the focus—or even mentioned.

  - How are you addressing their needs and their mission when they're second to your own? No judgment on others, just make an inventory of the discussions. I bet you'll be horrified.

- Discuss your insights with your colleagues without shaming anyone.

  - Acknowledge your own complicity.

  - Commit to a process or reminder system to pull the customer back front and center.

- Consider, in every applicable meeting, agreeing to spend five minutes talking about how the meeting topic relates to real, identified, verified customer needs.

  - Not every meeting needs to be customer-focused; discussing the company 401(k) plan is naturally inwardly focused. But the company holiday party, the annual President's Club trip, your next town hall—all of them could include time spent addressing and including an increased focus on your customer.

- Set a new (and short) recurring meeting, perhaps weekly and no longer than thirty minutes, to discuss only your customers. Each time an idea is introduced, ask these questions:

  - "How do we know that?"

- "Which customer told us that?"
- "Who did they tell it to?"

- If you had a war room, what would the sign currently say?

  - I'm guessing it would read: "Faster Growth," "Higher Margins," "Safety First," or "Eliminate Waste."
  - What would it say if you were insanely customer-focused?

CHALLENGE 2

MARKETING IS NOT JUST A DIVISION

Does everyone in your organization view marketing as siloed to you and your team, or do they understand they have a vital role to play as well?

Marketing should be the least siloed group in your organization.
Typically, divisions like finance, operations, supply chain, product development, and human resources are fairly insular. Since this isn't a book on organizational development, I won't opine on whether that's good or bad. My point is that marketing should be *everyone's* job, as opposed to sourcing vendors in Asia, setting payment terms with clients, or orienting new employees and managing benefits. I think these are generally best owned by their respective divisions.

Simply put, marketing is *everyone's* responsibility. And sure, there's generally a group of people organized into a team led by a CMO or VP, but stepping out of this marketing mess requires a different mindset. It's the shift from "Marketing owns the brand" to "Everyone owns the brand." Because if everyone doesn't feel like they own the brand, you're in trouble. This mindset draws from the similar adage "Everyone's in sales regardless of their role." So just swap out "marketing" for "sales" and you've got it—*everyone is in marketing, regardless of their role.*

At its simplest form, marketing is about building a brand buyers come to know, trust, purchase from and, ideally, tell others in their networks to purchase from as well. Every organization wants to achieve this as quickly, sustainably, and inexpensively as possible. One of the many ways to achieve this is by building brand ambassadors, also known as "rabid promoters," who evangelize your product or service at every possibility. According to Fred Richheld, the lead mind behind Bain's famous Net Promoter Score (NPS) system and the bestselling author of many books including *The Ultimate Question*, customers fall onto a 0–10 scale based on their loyalty to your brand. "Detractors" (0–6 on the NPS scale) are twice as likely to share a negative experience with friends and family as they are if they're considered "promoters" (9–10 on the NPS scale). FYI, 7s and 8s are classified as "passives." NPS has taken the world by storm in recent years, and for good reason. I think it has, perhaps unintentionally, raised the dialogue inside organizations about the value of not just external promoters but internal promoters as well, or of seeing your associates as treasured brand ambassadors.

Flip the script for a minute and look *inside* your organization at how many employees are treasured brand ambassadors that can be better developed to support your business growth. One year, during my tenure as the chief marketing officer at FranklinCovey, I joined our annual companywide kickoff and predictably moved off script. I spoke extemporaneously about how everyone in the room, including the thousand plus associates worldwide who had joined virtually, were all in fact "in marketing" as brand ambassadors. Although FranklinCovey has tens of thousands of valued clients, their United States sales force of about two hundred people meets face-to-face with twenty thousand current and prospective clients annually. Face-to-face encounters are the backbone of our sales strategy and are a key leading sales measure. In fact, they're so key to goal attainment and meeting budget and revenue commitments that algorithmically, we knew how much revenue, on average, comes from every hour spent with clients to mutual benefit. And your organization should do the same.

That's twenty thousand chances annually, in the United States alone, to create a positive experience with the brand. That's significant, but it pales in comparison when you think about the larger employee base that isn't directly in sales (I know, *everyone* is in sales, so just bear with me). I'm talking about every encounter with every employee, whether at dinner parties, summer picnics, industry conferences, casual conversations on flights and trains, or even social media posts on topics that have little to do with your organization's brand. We are all brand ambassadors in every interaction, and each is an opportunity to support or diminish our company's brand.

Years ago, I worked with a massive entertainment company that had an unbelievably strict policy: a "zero social media" directive for all employees. Let me repeat: as a condition of your employment, you were prohibited from engaging in any personal social media. None. Not just no posting, but no social media accounts, period. I suspect this has softened in the ensuing years, but it shows how seriously they protected their brand. I'm not suggesting you enact a similarly draconian policy, but instead recognize how something like reckless social posting can easily detract from—or worse, materially damage—your organization's brand. If you simply cast marketing as a separate division in your organization, where only some have the job as brand ambassadors, you're primed to step into a prickly mess. How many of your employees have social media profiles that include their employer, job title, and work contact info? Probably more than you think.

The frequent workplace videos popping up all over the internet are a CMO's worst nightmare. How do you bring a brand to its knees? Post a clip of a fast-food employee cleaning the restaurant tables with a mop previously used on the floor. Watch a video of a barista replacing a customer's name on a coffee cup with a racial slur. Or have an associate photocopy their *derrière* on the company copy machine and post the chef d'oeuvre on Instagram with the company sign displayed in the background. It never "ends" well (pun intended).

But it's not always so insidious.

Several years ago, a colleague of mine, a well-traveled professional, posted on her social media an excoriating rebuke of an airline that also happened to be our long-term client. For such an otherwise measured professional, I was incredulous when I read it. I couldn't believe "Tina" was trashing the airline's brand by insinuating the nearly one hundred thousand employees who work tirelessly to serve their valued customers were complicit in the unconscionable behavior of those caught on video treating a passenger beyond poorly. This organization didn't need our employee exacerbating the already horrible public relations nightmare. Remember, you're a brand ambassador of your employer whether you realize or like it.

I texted a photo of the post to our HR lead and they handled the communication with Tina quickly and appropriately. She was contrite and concurred about her own lapse in judgment, and Tina deleted the post shortly thereafter. In fact, I remember her now far more for how she responded to the feedback than for the post itself. Let's talk straight: we've all been there, including me. In the heat of the moment, we may make decisions and judgments about others and don't always rise to the standards we set for ourselves and our organization. It's only called hypocrisy if you *continue* to say one thing and do another. Be absolutely certain that you're practicing what you preach. And if you're ever called out, immediately acknowledge your incongruence. Don't defend yourself, but rather thank the other person for the reminder. Remember, we learn more from our own messes than from our successes.

One of the best strategies I know for moving from a marketing mess to brand success is to educate every associate in your organization, regardless of your size and reach, that how they behave is a direct reflection of your overall brand. Yes, it's a high standard; but like it or not, they're already acting as a potential detractor or powerful promoter.

I fly a lot, so I will draw on another airline example. Because of my status on Delta, I was recently invited to a small focus group that included seven very seasoned travelers. This airline, on which I have flown over two million miles, gathered the seven of us together for a meeting at the local airport lounge to ask us some pointed questions about their brand and our experiences with it. Delta had assembled about forty employees that included baggage handlers, ticket and gate agents, flight attendants, and even pilots. They posed questions that ranged from our opinions on their uniforms to how we liked their frequent-flyer benefits. I shared several sincere compliments about their service, but then also offered a criticism and pulled no punches in telling them that I was tired of hearing the flight crew complain about their own airline. And when I say complain, I mean the industry-wide experience every traveler witnesses sooner or later. It's the understandable and irresponsible moaning and lamenting I can easily hear if I'm seated in either the very front or very back of the plane near their jump seats. It's not building my loyalty to your airline when I hear you air your own legitimate complaints while I'm using your service. The conversations typically range from long layovers, unfulfilled schedule requests, or other annoyances that come with their often thankless roles. To all flight attendants: please know how much we genuinely appreciate your service, patience, humanity and, lamentably, the dignity you've lost to rude and selfish passengers. Whether you work for Nordstrom, Target, Taco Bell, or you're on staff at the local recreation center, we all have parts of our job we lament; let's just agree not to share them where the customer can hear them.

To Delta's credit, they not only validated my comment, but later discussed among themselves possible next steps to address the issue companywide. My already intense loyalty to this airline was increased that day. Let's just say on the NPS scale, for Delta, I'm an 11.

Everyone is in marketing, regardless of their role. Spread the word.

FROM MESS TO SUCCESS:

MARKETING IS NOT JUST A DIVISION

- Have a conversation with every associate to reinforce their role as a brand ambassador (beyond what's been communicated in the compulsory policy manual).

  - Articulate what being a brand ambassador looks and sounds like.

  - Review behavior standards that apply to everyone in the organization, including the CEO.

  - Show some of the now infamous videos and social posts that illustrate the brand fallout that can happen from simple jokes or unintended actions. Conversely, share some of the videos and examples of when an employee went beyond the call of duty and, unbeknownst to them, it was witnessed and recorded by others and became a viral brand boost. Remember, everyone's now a movie producer, camera in hand, and has global distribution at their fingertips.

- Talk about proactive efforts associates can engage in to build the brand and even easily promote your products and services, including:

  - Making it affordable for associates to use, wear, and even distribute your products and services to their networks. Setting some preapproved guidelines can also shrink or eliminate employee theft.

  - Discussing the "undiscussables," such as dress, hygiene, and other reasonable protocols related to representing your brand well. Morals and standards clauses are increasingly common beyond the C-suite.

- Focus on building a winning culture—a place where people love to come because they are challenged, respected, and given the freedom to take reasonable risks that stretch their skills. Associates who feel trusted and trust their employer (and their direct leaders) are more loyal and protective, often intentionally choosing to "talk up" their organization. Pride in association is an undeniable motivator.

CHALLENGE 3

STAY CLOSE TO THE CASH

Are you an integral part of the cash-generating machine?

Disclaimer: Do not confuse the title of this challenge with success by association. Let me be uberclear: "Stay close to the cash" means you're a noticeably vital part of the cash-generating machine, not merely a hanger-on trying to professionally "photobomb" those who are.

I was in Trinidad at a company conference when the call came in from the chief people officer, rarely something anyone looks forward to—the call, I mean; not my being in Trinidad. He was actually reaching out on behalf of our CEO to discuss a formal announcement: I was to be named to the company's executive team as an "NEO," Named Executive Officer. Quite the honor, and a lot of responsibility in a publicly traded company. Not only does the CEO make this decision, but the board of directors must then approve it. As a result, your name goes on record with the Securities and Exchange Commission making you responsible (and liable) for a slew of decisions. It was a big deal to me, and I took it very seriously.

With the same seriousness that I approached the promotion, I considered my new title. I definitely didn't want to become the executive vice president of marketing. I'd been in the firm at that point long enough to have lived through a myriad of marketing vice presidents, and none seem to have lasted more than two years—a time frame not unique to our company.

In a recent study analyzing tenure in the C-suite, Korn Ferry, the executive recruiting firm, reported that of all C-suite positions, the CEO tends to be the longest-tenured. The average length of a CEO's tenure is 5.3 years. Conversely, the CMO (tied with the CIO) has the shortest at 4.1 years. Yikes!

I wasn't privy to *why* exactly, but from the outside looking in, it appeared as if these former vice presidents of marketing were too focused on *marketing*.

Huh?

What's wrong with that you ask? I know, it seems fairly straightforward that a vice president of marketing should be focused on marketing. But therein lies the problem. A vice president of marketing should be equally focused on *sales*! You know, small things like recruiting and retaining revenue-generating clients that put cash in the bank. For fear of patronizing any of you, here's a disclaimer: I'm confident you know and are dedicating the focus of your marketing career to the primary outcome of marketing: revenue. But I intend to be a bit demonstrative in my reminder because it's so easy when you have the "marketing" moniker in your title to just focus on classic marketing tasks like building brand equity, creating impressions, designing logos, writing copy for brochures, producing webinars, creating social posts, etc.

The risk, of course, is that you can find yourself being quickly disconnected, or worse, disassociated from the lifeblood of any business: cash. Stay as close to the cash as humanly possible. The marketing leaders prior to me who had taken their brief turn at the helm seemed to be missing that palpable craving for direct revenue responsibility. In fact, most stayed as far away from owning a revenue goal as possible! For those of you who still feel I've just offered sophomoric advice, here's a litmus test: The next time you walk past the executive suite and you see the CFO or vice president of finance sitting with the CEO and the door is closed, don't assume they're talking about the next acquisition. They may well be discussing the reality of having only a three-week runway of cash left in the bank and the pending impossibility of fully funding next month's payroll. If you're not sitting in that meeting with them, it's because you're not viewed as part of the solution, but rather as part of the problem. A bit dramatic I know, but you get the point: Build your marketing brand as a vital part of the cash-generating machine.

I've probably offended some of you reading this. But if you have the courage to keep going, check your ego for a moment and think about this truth objectively. I think most will agree that marketing is a safer career than sales—until sales underperforms, quickly sells out marketing, and the CEO turns marketing out on the street. If you think this was just a funny throwaway line in this chapter, it's not—it's exactly the cycle most companies follow. Too many "marketers" are in marketing because it seemed like a great outlet for their creative energy and ideas, allowing them to be safely distanced from managing (or understanding) a profit-and-loss statement (P&L), and, most vitally, from owning revenue responsibility. I'm certain my longevity in the CMO position is less related to my genius marketing skills and creativity (both of which are probably hotly debated by former team members) and more to the fact that I aligned myself so closely to owning and closing the quarters—right alongside the sales division.

I truly believe this is what set me apart from the many competent marketing leaders before me. And to those of them reading this, I certainly hope you know I understand the complexities of owning marketing inside any organization and fully recognize that all of you have thrived elsewhere. This chapter isn't to throw any of you under the bus, but to illustrate how easy it is to end up in a marketing mess when you don't seek to co-own sales.

Some of my proudest moments in the seven years I served as FranklinCovey's first and only chief marketing officer and the EVP of business development were when the chairman & CEO assigned me projects as if I were the EVP of *sales*. Sometimes it was a bit awkward because the highly competent EVP of sales was often sitting at the same table as me. But when the CEO is assigning revenue responsibility and asking for results on a sales campaign from the CMO, it shows great confidence that marketing and sales are not only aligned and working in tandem toward the same goals, but have demonstrably rejected the notion that they must always be at odds.

A quick aside: The EVP of sales at the time was immensely capable and a personal friend of mine. Our revenue, profitability, share price, and impact on clients grew substantially under his sales leadership. He and I worked in tandem on every campaign—we didn't always perfectly agree in private, but in public, we executed better than Sonny and Cher, or a closer-to-home metaphor in Salt Lake City, the famed Jazz basketball duo Stockton and Malone. For those of you who aren't basketball aficionados, one of the most famous NBA pronouncements was "Stockton to Malone!" which indicated John Stockton had set the ball up for his often-better-known teammate, Karl Malone, to dunk it in. I was proud to be the Stockton (marketing) to the Malone (sales). The CEO didn't confuse my responsibility to include revenue because the sales EVP was incompetent.

The opposite, in fact. He simply had high trust in our skills and relationship to deliver together. Look to create your own dynamic duo with your sales counterpart, and the organization will be unstoppable.

Had I been aware of the Korn Ferry data regarding CMO tenure prior to beginning the job, it might have created some pause in my acceptance. Nah, who am I kidding? I love adversity. But what I love more is being relevant, and I nearly doubled the 4.1-year CMO average, in part because I learned to avoid the trappings of a marketing mess by challenging the conventional wisdom of marketing and my role leading it.

Stay close to the cash.

Now, I'm quite certain some of you think I'm a capitalistic pig because I somehow turned the third chapter of my marketing book into one all about cash. Nothing will deter me from the undeniable fact that *every* organization needs cash to progress their mission and fulfill their promises and obligations to their customers and stakeholders. This includes nonprofits, ecclesiastical organizations, educational institutions, GMOs, and the backbone of every economy, for-profit enterprises. My finest day will be when the sales leader reading this book hands it to the marketing leader, or even better, when the marketing leader cascades it on to their marketing team members. Staying close to the cash means you are actively cogenerating cash with sales, and you feel as responsible for it as they do. To quote my dear friend and renowned sales leader Marianne Phillips, "Get in my boat and row with me."

Those who are closely aligned with revenue get cut last. Be the person in your organization most vitally associated with generating cash, and you will always have not merely a job, but a relevant career.

FROM MESS TO SUCCESS:

STAY CLOSE TO THE CASH

- Ask yourself why you've chosen a career in marketing? What do you believe that really means in terms of your contribution to the cash-generating machine?

- If you haven't proactively chosen a marketing role but ended up with it as an additional responsibility, how will you fine-tune your marketing and business acumen to ensure relevance when it's potentially not your real passion or area of expertise?

- Challenge your marketing-role paradigm.

  - Are you hiding from revenue responsibility in the marketing department?

  - Why are you in marketing instead of sales, product development, or some other role or division?

  - What's your contribution beyond traditional (and important) marketing activities to ensure the long-term growth and viability of your company?

  - Ask yourself on a daily or hourly basis, *How is what I'm working on now ensuring cash generation for the company?*

  - How will you insulate yourself from the winds of change (a.k.a. the whims of the C-suite) when they need to cut costs or change strategy?

CHALLENGE 4

BECOME THE LEADER OF BUSINESS DEVELOPMENT

Are you humble enough to recognize the role marketing must play in service of sales?

There are some subtle but important differences between the concepts outlined in Challenge 3 ("Stay Close to the Cash") and what I intend to address now. It will be vital to challenge your mindset about what it means to be in marketing and how that responsibility drives sales. Understanding your organization's culture and what is prioritized (and not being offended or emboldened by it) is paramount to you and your team's success. Subtle changes in titles, division names, and mindsets can have a substantial impact on your relevance and longevity. Enter this chapter thinking about changes in your own belief system about sales and marketing, and in your organization's growth engine, that might best serve everyone involved. In my case, I was always introduced as the chief marketing officer, but I always operated through the lens of executive vice president of business development.

Previously, I shared that when asked to join my company's executive team, I didn't want to be the executive vice president of marketing. I could rattle off the names of a half-dozen people who'd preceded me with very short and less than memorable tenures. I was determined to change that pattern and avoid getting stuck in the proverbial marketing mess.

Fortunately for me, my advancement marked the first time in the firm's history when the marketing role was elevated to the executive team, so it provided a level of implied longevity, as CEOs of public companies are often loath to change officers without significant cause. As such, during my promotion, I was invited to weigh in on my complete title. I suggested adding to "chief marketing officer" the title of "executive vice president of business development."

Truth be told, I didn't really want to own marketing; instead, I wanted to own business development as the *outcome* of marketing—perhaps a subtle yet important difference in how I wanted the contribution of our team to be perceived across the company. I was determined to make it very clear to everyone in the firm (at the time, we had offices in fifty-plus countries, and more at the time of this writing) that our responsibility was to fill the pipeline for sales. And I was delighted, honored even, to be held to account. Yes, we would also be responsible for the brand, logos, messaging, public relations, digital properties, product launches, etc. But what I really wanted to impact was revenue and profitability. One way to avoid a marketing mess is to acknowledge that marketing *is already* on the line for business-development outcomes, whether overtly articulated or not. The surest way to accomplish that is to have some control and ownership over what you're already responsible for. Personally, I love clear accountability and thrive under revenue pressure. I suspect that having inherited my mother's Methodist/Protestant work ethic and my father's Catholic guilt has served me well after all.

Because I formally included business development as part of my role, our team quickly became indispensable to the CEO. Some of my colleagues even intimated that they often saw me as his most valued team member because of my unusual willingness to be accountable for revenue while in a marketing role. Before long, the marketing team grew from three people to over thirty, and not because the CEO and CFO loved to spend money on the black hole often known as marketing. The team grew because we proved to them and the board of directors that we were not merely a cost center but a revenue center—one vital to the lifeblood of sales. The fact of the matter is that both the CEO and the CFO were quite willing to increase the company's marketing spend. They just needed a higher level of assurance that precious investments wouldn't be lost in marketing's pet projects, but rather would be indisputably tied to increasing client outcomes and consequentially bring in more revenue. We even merged with several other revenue centers and, as a result, I had direct P&L responsibility for even more revenue channels. Certainly not typical for a CMO, but it's also not typical to last nearly eight years in that position either.

Every organization has a different culture in terms of their growth engine. P&G, Nike, Oracle, Apple, Intel, Salesforce, and Coca-Cola all have well-known engines that dominate their internal cultures. Some focus on innovation and research, others on brand or marketing, and still others see sales as king. Obviously, they all need sales to thrive. But their success comes from focusing a good deal of their time, energy, and resources on other areas that drive sales. Sales is not always the primary engine of a culture, and I think it often turns on the comfort, background, and competence of the CEO and where they prefer to spend their own time and talents.

I'll write more about the vital relationship between sales and marketing later in the book, but for this challenge, I want to state this important lesson: When I was promoted to become CMO, I was equal to every other position on the team, aside from the CFO and CEO. I could have come to the table with some swagger and built an empire (I'm sure some think I tried) and attempted to tip the balance from sales to marketing. I consciously did the opposite, thinking and behaving like I *reported* to sales, even though I clearly did not. I reported to the CEO just like the sales leader did. I intentionally deferred to my peer, the EVP of sales, on most occasions, and saw my job as supporting his efforts.

"Stockton to Malone!"

An important caveat about me is that I rarely, if ever, defer to anyone. I've got skills and I know it. I've also got abounding humility (said by nobody who does). Let's just say it wasn't easy for me, but I knew aligning closely to sales would ultimately serve both our clients and our organization, and build the relevance of our broader team. This ultimately built a culture of synergy and collaboration, and in the process grew careers that have flourished for many.

Those responsible for marketing who want to avoid a common mess must learn to support sales and not compete. The former EVP of sales and I are dear friends to this day, both with strong opinions and differences. He would likely say my support was crucial to the significant increase in sales and client successes we experienced. It was a mindset I intentionally chose and then aligned my behaviors with daily. Had he not been competent, this story would be very different. That mindset and the behaviors I modeled permeated the entire marketing division, but not always to everyone's delight.

Midway through my tenure as CMO and EVP of business development, I hired an associate from outside the company to join the division. Our culture, like every organization, isn't always easy to assimilate into for a senior outside hire. Extremely technically competent, this new colleague and I were like oil and water interpersonally. Welcome to high achievers. That never really bothered either of us, I think; I love a good debate and I suspect he did too. Where we often found ourselves sideways with each other was when I would reinforce to the entire marketing division that our role was to support sales and that "sales is king and they pay our salaries." This simply rubbed him the wrong way, which I suspect I knew and so kept doing because I'm petty at times. To see just how petty I can be, read my first book, *Management Mess to Leadership Success: 30 Challenges to Become the Leader You Would Follow.*

My point in making such a declaration to the marketing team was to also communicate that we have no right to exist. We have to earn and reearn it daily (just like they do in sales), but at the end of the day, nothing happens or gets funded until someone sells something. This mindset of mine was a major contention point for this colleague, as I think he believed I was dishonoring marketing and minimizing our role and overall contribution. That simply was not the case. I chose a career in marketing by leaving a decade-long successful career in sales and sales leadership. As the leader, I'd worked wisely and tirelessly to build a powerful team of "A" players who were now highly relevant in the organization. Nobody before me had accomplished this in our nearly forty-year history. Their salaries were highly competitive, and the CEO knew them all by name. My respect for every marketing associate was palpable, but at the end of the day, it was important to recognize that our role was to be fixated on helping sales achieve their goals and revenue commitments, and it was healthy to keep that fact top of mind for all of our team members. I suspect my belief system is grounded in the previous decade I'd spent on the sales side of our organization, knowing how difficult a sales role can be, especially when you don't have a marketing team fiercely focused on your success. I have zero regrets... at least not about that mindset anyway.

I'm sure by now you think I am beyond fixated with supporting sales, revenue, and cash.

You're damn right I am.

But I'm also appreciative of all the other important areas marketing is responsible for, including the organization's reputation, maintaining consistent brand standards, building evergreen digital properties, optimizing SEO, creating relevant sales tools, building marketing funnels, and dozens of other agile processes and systems. Marketing's contribution to any organization can be incalculable. Your ongoing challenge is to balance your day job—all those things I just mentioned—with a fierce and palpable contribution to business development and its immediate connection to sales.

FROM MESS TO SUCCESS:

BECOME THE LEADER OF BUSINESS DEVELOPMENT

- Recognize that brand is invaluable, but you can't deposit it into the bank and fund payroll from it.

  - Determine if you're using "brand equity" conversations as air cover to perpetuate your safe marketing activities and keep them far from the lifeblood (revenue and cash) of the organization.

- Check your ego and better align marketing's functions (and your own skills) to support sales.

  - Determine the small but vital changes you can make to declare your intent to co-own sales/business development while being willing, if necessary, to strategically and mentally subordinate to it.

- Ask the questions you should be asking but likely aren't.

  - Do you have the organization's revenue goals committed to memory?

  - Does every member of your team know them as well?

  - Do you know daily, weekly, monthly, and quarterly how the organization is performing financially?

  - What measures are sales struggling to meet and exceed; and how, specifically, can marketing address them?

  - Is the CEO confusing marketing with sales in a good way? What could you do to create more of that positive confusion (without hijacking or undermining the sales leader's role, which could erode trust if done with bad intent)?

- Can you demonstrate, without puffery or scraping the bottom of the barrel, how marketing is *driving*, not just supporting, business development?

- Do you possess the humility and vulnerability to meet with your leader, or the leader of sales, and have a candid conversation on what exactly the marketing division or team could do to measurably increase their support?

CHALLENGE 5

UNDERSTAND AND
DEFINE YOUR CHARTER

*Do you have a plan, or are you willing
to be a part of someone else's?*

An author and dear friend of mine, Dr. Blaine Lee, said, "Nearly all, if not all conflict in life comes from mismatched or unfulfilled expectations." I share this often on podcasts, interviews, and in keynote speeches. It's truly profound if you sit and stew on it. Think about all the conflict in your life, with your leader, sales vice president, inner-division colleagues, clients, neighbors, handyman, roofer, your spouse or partner, your children, or your mother-in-law. Most, if not all, of such messes can be minimized or outright eliminated with enough clarity on the front side of the project, meeting, high-stakes conversation, or holiday plans. Rarely do interpersonal issues become clearer with neglect.

Where is Thanksgiving dinner being hosted again this year? Of course, at your super rich and successful know-it-all brother-in-law's, because you've never sat him (and your sister) down and talked straight about your own dreams for hosting the event at your much smaller home without a fourth bathroom or fully tricked-out game room. The same happens in our organizations. As marketing professionals, it's imperative we practice straight talk with our leaders about understanding our charter—what exactly is expected from marketing? What does success look like? What are the specific measures within our control to ensure we're delivering the results we've signed up for? And in some organizations, depending on the culture, it might be that the leader you report to isn't exactly sure what to expect from marketing, and you may need to take the proverbial bull by the horns and define your own charter for them.

When leading marketing initiatives, which by their nature tend to have nebulous results, you can avoid a common marketing mess by directly clarifying expectations—sometimes even beyond the point of reason. Do you fully understand what's expected from you and your team? What exactly have you been charged with accomplishing, and when and how will you both know when that's been achieved? Marketing is fraught with mismatched expectations. It's absolutely your responsibility to clarify what success looks like, and if your leader isn't sure or happens to be confused themselves, this becomes your responsibility and opportunity to rise to the challenge and lead by boldly offering your own plans and ensuring you both end up perfectly aligned. Absent you taking the initiative, you're highly likely to be headed toward confusion, disappointment, and missed expectations—in other words, a marketing mess. Don't confuse their confidence with expertise; when you do, you may well sign up for unachievable goals and when you miss them, you'll be left holding the bag.

Let's dive into a marketing mess we can all learn from. I recall an especially creative campaign from the marketing division (long before my tenure as the CMO). At the time, I was a sales leader, and marketing developed a campaign to send a very large box of chocolates to prospective clients with a certain percentage of the chocolates missing. The number of absent chocolates correlated to one of our research findings. In this case, it illustrated the percentage of employees who didn't fully understand or couldn't even name the most important goals of their organization, and thus the box was less than fifty percent filled with chocolates. Included in the box was a note inviting the recipient to engage with the firm and learn how to "fill in" the rest. If a prospective client reached out, the marketing team would mail the rest of the chocolates to them in the hopes of beginning a conversation that the sales team could follow up on. I thought it was quite inventive and original, but that wasn't a popular position to share.

I recall the naïve marketing team coming in to woo us arrogant sales jerks; they left with mixed expectations and varying levels of support. Soon after, the deployment of thousands of boxes of chocolates to prospective clients began. Think of the carpet-bombing raids of World War II, only instead of explosives, we were covering the corporate landscape in chocolate. Marketing was beaming with pride at all of this (and truth be told, so was I across the aisle in sales, but I couldn't share that with my peers, or we might be complicit when it failed). It reminded me of a newly elected freshman congressman excited to reach across the aisle to a member of the other party and having that idea crushed early on by their party whip. "How dare you collaborate? What are you, *sane* or something?"

Operation Willy Wonka failed, and the sales team was further validated. Not only were the expectations far from being effectively communicated early on, marketing came to sales with a fully baked idea ready to implement. Imagine for a moment if sales had been a part of that process from the beginning—if marketing had interviewed us about the goals we wanted to focus on, how to best accomplish them, and what types of campaigns we would agree to so everyone had skin in the game—and if, regardless of the results, "we were all in it together." But this didn't happen, and the only people to benefit were the doctors performing diabetes tests.

So here's the point: Invest the time and patience to listen to the needs of the business while leaving your ego at the door. What exact results does the organization expect from marketing? What is your charter and has it been communicated to the broader organization so everyone understands what marketing *is* and *isn't* responsible for delivering? I'm repeating it again: What is your charter? To innovate? collaborate? brainstorm? Have you clarified marketing's level of empowerment and permission to be independently creative? Every culture has nuances, but is marketing's role to think up a variety of campaigns and then present them to sales? Or are sales and marketing combined into one division, with everything to be done lockstep together without independent brainstorming? Are you to focus on brand awareness with the eighteen hundred school district superintendents or drive to twenty-four face-to-face meetings with purchasing directors by the end of this month? Is your responsibility to build a new web presence and implement a nurture track for inbound inquires, or to secure twelve of your competitor's clients in a live webinar by the end of the quarter?

I can't help but think short CMO tenure is somewhat correlated to mismatched expectations between the CMO and the CEO, and most certainly between the CMO and the CRO (Chief Revenue Officer). I think it's easier for the CEO to push out (i.e., fire) the CMO than the CRO in most organizations when the numbers aren't delivering. Were those enough acronyms for you? Sales divisions are typically more entrenched than the marketing department, and it's usually marketing that becomes the "fall guy" when sales misses their number. Understanding and defining your charter proactively will help inoculate yourself and your marketing team members from this corporate cultural phenomenon.

Want to avoid this marketing mess? Don't become a solution looking for a problem. Instead, check your ego and ask what's needed. Don't be afraid to push back when it seems delusional (and at times it will). Be thoughtful. This doesn't mean you're always disagreeing or negotiating, because that's absolutely the wrong paradigm. I never negotiated outcomes with the CEO. Because if I won, that meant I was likely underperforming against his original expectations by making him agree to a lower standard than he wanted. If I won, I lost.

Instead, show confidence and reason while you talk through what's possible and, candidly, what's not. Find out what's a bold stretch but still attainable. At the end of the discussion(s), be sure you're both clear on your charter. Often in such a conversation with the CEO, I would ask, "Can you tell me exactly how much revenue you are holding me (and our marketing team) accountable for with this campaign?" I would then leave the meeting clear that I owed $380,000 in revenue by the end of the quarter directly from our marketing efforts. Or sometimes it was $3.8 million. Either was fine; I just needed clarity on our charter to avoid a marketing mess.

Please take note: If the above question scares you, then you shouldn't be in marketing.

CEOs respect and retain marketers who aren't afraid to own or co-own the revenue outcome. Perhaps your outcome won't be revenue-focused, and that's fine. At least you're clear on your charter. I think that single principle kept me in the role more than any other skill or talent.

If you own or work for marketing in an organization where there isn't a bounty of self-appointed experts (cherish that), then be bold in articulating a charter, which may include your vision, strategy, and outcomes independent of a clear directive. Your charter may in fact relate to revenue. And if that's the case, announce something like: "This omnichannel campaign will include direct mail, email, podcast and radio interviews, follow-up calls, and other promos, and we will deliver 240 registrations to the spring virtual conference, resulting in tuition of $71,760 by the end of the early-bird deadline." If the number isn't 240 but rather 24, then state it so everyone is clear on what they're signing up for. Simultaneously, clarify your budget and the intervals in which you'll report progress or concerns so everyone works together toward a common, articulated goal.

FROM MESS TO SUCCESS:

UNDERSTAND AND DEFINE YOUR CHARTER

- Become more self-aware about your general level of guessing in life.

  - Are you operating on facts or inferences? Don't confuse your emotions, feelings, and opinions with facts. Both are valuable and both are very different.

  - Consider what could happen if you moved further outside your comfort zone and asked a few more clarifying questions to uncover any gaps in your own and someone else's expectations.

- Take control of the conversation with your leader as it relates to clarifying your charter.

  - Set a meeting and say something like: "Hey, I'd like to check in with you and clarify the different projects we're working on. I want to be certain we're directly aligned to your priorities, as I know things shift and I want our team to be extremely relevant. Would you mind if I reviewed what I think are our current priorities, and I welcome you to challenge any of them so we can recalibrate our focus if necessary?"

- Exercise the maturity, wisdom, and sound judgment to establish your own charter if there is no clear direction from your leader.

  - Test and benchmark your charter against others in the organization whose feedback would be valuable prior to presenting it to your leader for consideration.

- Ensure that every necessary stakeholder has agreed to and bought in to your marketing commitments so everyone owns the successes and failures (there will be both).

- Identify areas in your life where there's interpersonal conflict.

  - Consider how clarifying expectations could not only lessen or eliminate the stress, but even build higher trust in the process and person.

CHALLENGE 6

DECIDE YOUR OWN TENURE

Are you willing to disrupt your own career before it's disrupted for you?

I'm privileged to host a weekly podcast for FranklinCovey called *On Leadership with Scott Miller.* And yes, I'm going to plug it and invite you to subscribe. *On Leadership* has grown to become the world's largest weekly newsletter and podcast dedicated to the topic of leadership. FranklinCovey's superb production team and I host experts, bestselling authors, CEOs, and thought leaders every Tuesday, providing a platform for their perspectives and insights.

Of our first 150 guests, I clearly have some favorites (sorry, not divulging), but at the risk of sounding hyperbolic, each one has added value to my own career and skill development. Any wisdom I've gained in my personal and professional life is directly the result of learning from someone who has stepped out in front of me either through their own risk taking, research, or willingness to share their own messes. I can't begin to express my full appreciation to this collection of thought leaders for joining us on this weekly series.

At the time of publication, here's a list of On *Leadership* guests and their topics:

Stephen M. R. Covey	*The Speed of Trust*
Susan Cain	*Quiet: The Power of Introverts in a World That Can't Stop Talking*
Todd Davis	*Get Better: 15 Proven Practices to Building Effective Relationships at Work*
Liz Wiseman	*Multipliers*
Kory Kogon	*The 5 Choices to Extraordinary Productivity*
Hyrum Smith	*What Matters Most*
Daniel Amen, MD	*Change Your Brain, Change Your Life*

Sandy Rogers	*Leading Loyalty*
Daniel Pink	*When: The Scientific Secrets of Perfect Timing*
Suzette Blakemore	*Project Management for the Unofficial Project Manager*
Seth Godin	*This Is Marketing*
Chris McChesney	*The 4 Disciplines of Execution*
Eric Barker	*Barking Up the Wrong Tree*
Sean Covey	*The 7 Habits of Highly Effective Teens*
Leena Rinne	*The 5 Choices to Extraordinary Productivity*
Nancy Duarte	*slide:ology*
David Sibbet & Gisela Wendling	*Visual Consulting*
Doris Kearns Goodwin	*Leadership in Turbulent Times*
Karen Dillon	*How Will You Measure Your Life*
Marché Barney	*Presentation and Facilitation Tips*
Dewitt Jones	*The Nature of Leadership*
General Stanley McChrystal	*Leaders: Myth and Reality*
Nely Galán	*Self Made*
Anne Chow	*CEO, AT&T Business*
Jennifer Colosimo	*The 7 Habits of Highly Effective People*

Lonnie Moore & Gary McGuey	*Senior Education Consultants, FranklinCovey*
Julie Morgenstern	*Time to Parent*
Dorie Clark	*Stand Out*
Whitney Johnson	*Disrupt Yourself*
Randy Illig	*Let's Get Real or Let's Not Play*
Susan David, PhD	*Emotional Agility*
Shawn Moon	*Talent Unleashed*
Laura Vanderkam	*What the Most Successful People Do Before Breakfast*
Guy Kawasaki	*Wise Guy*
Pamela Fuller	*Unconscious Bias*
Stephanie McMahon	*WWE, Chief Brand Officer*
Bob Whitman	*Chairman & CEO, FranklinCovey*
Marissa Orr	*Lean Out*
Curtis Jones, PhD	*2019 School Superintendent of the Year*
Gretchen Rubin	*Outer Order, Inner Calm*
Aaron Thompson	*Director of Recruitment, FranklinCovey*
Kim Scott	*Radical Candor*
Donald Miller	*Building a Story Brand*

Jean Chatzky	*Women with Money*
Julian Treasure	*How to Be Heard*
Muriel Summers	*National Blue Ribbon School Principal*
Howard Ross	*Everyday Bias*
Jay Papasan	*The ONE Thing*
Bill Engvall	*Comedian, Blue Collar Comedy*
Paul White, PhD	*The 5 Languages of Appreciation in the Workplace*
Victoria Roos Olsson	*Everyone Deserves a Great Manager*
Chester Elton	*The Best Team Wins*
Jon Gordon	*The Energy Bus*
Michael Hyatt	*Free to Focus*
Leif Babin	*Extreme Ownership*
Patty McCord	*Powerful*
David Epstein	*Range*
Tererai Trent, PhD	*The Awakened Woman*
Daniel Coyle	*The Culture Code*
Geoffrey Moore	*Crossing the Chasm*
Julie Zhuo	*The Making of a Manager*
Rachel Hollis	*Girl, Wash Your Face*

Diana O'Brien	*Global Chief Marketing Officer, Deloitte US*
Kristen Ulmer	*The Art of Fear*
Tom Rath	*Life's Great Question*
Joel Peterson	*Entrepreneurial Leadership*
Nir Eyal	*Indistractable*
Ryan Holiday	*Stillness Is the Key*
Shawn Achor	*The Happiness Advantage*
Marie Forleo	*Everything Is Figureoutable*
Dave Hollis	*Get Out of Your Own Way*
Turia Pitt	*Unmasked*
Mark Manson	*The Subtle Art of Not Giving a F*ck*
Rita McGrath	*Seeing Around Corners*
Elizabeth Smart	*My Story*
Ed Mylett	*#MaxOut Your Life*
Tiffany Shlain	*24/6: The Power of Unplugging One Day a Week*
John Gray	*Men Are from Mars, Women Are from Venus*
Trent Shelton	*The Greatest You*
Stedman Graham	*Identity Leadership*
Greg Moore	*Co-Chair Pulitzer Prize Committee*

John Maxwell	*The Leader's Greatest Return*
Jack Canfield	*Chicken Soup for the Soul*
Tasha Eurich	*Insight*
Bobby Herrera	*The Gift of Struggle*
Janice Bryant Howroyd	*Acting Up*
Nick Vujicic	*Life Without Limits*
Mike Koenigs	*Cancerprenuer*
Adam Davidson	*The Passion Economy*
BJ Fogg	*Tiny Habits*
Brendon Burchard	*High Performance Habits*
Dov Baron	*Fiercely Loyal*
Wanda Wallace	*You Can't Know It All*
Janice Kaplan	*The Genius of Women*
Madeline Levine	*Ready or Not*
M.J. Fievre	*Badass Black Girl*
Laird Hamilton	*Liferider*
David Rubenstein	*How to Lead*
Patrick Bet-David	*Your Next Five Moves*
Peter Winick	*Founder of Thought Leadership Leverage*

Chris Hogan	*Everyday Millionaires*
Alex Osterwalder	*Business Model Generation*
Mauro Guillén	*2030*
Ozan Varol	*Think Like a Rocket Scientist*
Tobias Beck	*Unbox Your Life*
Haydn Shaw	*Sticking Points*
Michael Simpson, Kari Saddler, Maria Sullivan	*Unlocking Potential*
Matthew McConaughey	*Greenlights*

If you weren't convinced by my previous plug to subscribe to the podcast, I hope you are now, after reviewing the enormously valuable collection of interviews with transformative insights into leadership, marketing, organizational culture, building high-performance teams, and developing trustworthy interpersonal relationships. Plus, all the interviews are archived at FranklinCovey.com, and you can watch or listen to them at your leisure.

One of our *On Leadership* interviewees, Whitney Johnson, inspired my thinking on the topic of deciding your own tenure. Whitney is a renowned innovation and disruption expert and the author of several books including *Disrupt Yourself: Master Relentless Change and Speed Up Your Learning Curve*. In our interview, we talked extensively about the changing landscape of career loyalty. Whitney shared her seven variables of career disruption, and I found number four, *battle entitlement*, to be most valuable. Her book challenges you to disrupt yourself before you're disrupted. Which you will be—it's not a question of *if*, but rather *when*. It's a superb read and I highly recommend it.

My father, who at the time of this writing is eighty-four, retired at age fifty-seven and has lived to enjoy nearly three decades of retirement. Like many in his generation at the onset of the digital revolution, he became disrupted. He'd invested thirty-four years of his career at Martin Marietta, a defense contractor that later became Lockheed Martin after a merger in the 1990s. As a draftsman, he worked with pencils and paper for over three decades; computer-aided design (CAD) and Apple's industry-disrupting software packages upended tens of thousands of talented artists just like him. It'd been a superb run and he transitioned to the best of his capabilities, but at some point, the gig was up.

Like father, like son.

It's been ingrained in me to be loyal to my employer and build my career inside one organization. I've worked for FranklinCovey for just shy of twenty-five years, and although I've had plenty of outside overtures, I've thoroughly enjoyed my tenure and feel both valued and well compensated for my contribution. As I look at my high school peers on social media, it seems to me that unless they're in the military or work for the United States Postal Service, specific careers inside the same organization are closer to five to eight years, max. And even *that* seems like an eternity to the newer generation flooding the workforce, who on average see twenty-four to thirty-six months as a career. I have palm fronds from Palm Sunday mass that are older than three years (likely because I was folding them into tiny crosses to keep my three sons engaged during an especially uninspiring homily, perhaps known as a sermon to some). But still, *three* years? Whitney Johnson believes that most professionals also have, regardless of what generation they hail from, about a three-year attention span for any one particular job. After three years, we tend to get bored, anxious, or ready to move to a new challenge—ideally, for some of us still inside our current organization. Her findings don't suggest we're ready to always leave our employer; we just need a new challenge in a new role.

Which begs the question: What's your plan? How long do you intend to be in your marketing role?

Increasingly, a goal of organizations is to build a culture where people can in fact fulfill most, if not all, of their career needs inside, not outside. For smaller companies and nonprofits, such a cultural goal is not always feasible. I've come to believe that too many marketing professionals put zero thought into their finish date. I am not one of them. I have, by and large, decided my own tenure in every job I've held. Some might even call me obsessed by it. To quote a friend of mine, Jon Acuff, who authored the book *Finish: Give Yourself the Gift of Done,* "Perfection is the enemy of completion." How often do we feel that we've finished our contribution, but our leaders above us aren't in agreement? Does your leader have the same opinion of your success and sense of completion as you do? Awareness of this disconnect can save you and them a lot of angst and awkward conversations.

With intentional focus, I have left nearly every job I've ever had at my own behest. I'd like to delude myself into thinking I was always earning myself a promotion, because that's what shows best on my LinkedIn profile. But the fact is, I've avoided a series of career messes by being wise enough to stay one step ahead of the proverbial boot—even if it meant a lateral move. Adopting such a mindset can help keep you relevant, and is also the exact opposite of what some of my colleagues did who've absolutely overstayed their tenure in their current roles. Even without the threat of a job-ending boot making contact with their backsides, they still managed to overstay their welcome. Often to the tune of years. Here's the hard truth: *You can't possibly stay fresh in the same role indefinitely.*

Many who find themselves in such a mess have accepted the veneer of confidence and security over the uncertainty of change. They're simply too scared to move on, move up, or move out. I get it, you've got obligations, bills, and commitments, and you've worked really hard to land in your current marketing role. Why would you ever think of giving it up? You've also probably suffered under some pretty torturous leaders in the process, and for those of you who are now the leader, you intend to squat as long as possible. But that's the mess that's waiting for your complacency. To avoid it, don't overstay your value.

Another one of my favorite interviews from the *On Leadership* podcast series was a conversation with Patty McCord, the former chief talent officer at Netflix and author of the book *Powerful*. Patty is one of the contributors to the famous Netflix Culture Deck, which sets forth the structure, values, and principles with which Netflix runs its organization. During our conversation, Patty challenged all leaders to exercise the courage to proactively disrupt members of their teams when their current role demands more than the skills they have to offer. Disrupt them when the effort it would take the individual to match the demands of their job is too much of a stretch or might end in a protracted failure or disappointment on all sides. In her straight-talk style, Patty impressed upon me what a humane gift it is to save someone from the potential humiliation of struggling in a role—or worse, hanging on and becoming the division pariah.

As I've reflected deeply on Patty's well-earned insights, I took her advice to heart and disrupted myself out of the chief marketing officer role (which I describe in Challenge 17: "Hire People Smarter Than You"). You've heard the adage that eventually everyone is promoted to the level of their own incompetence? Hmm… that hit close to home! What Patty offers is the antidote for when that happens to all of us. The reason I've included this chapter in a book about marketing is that, of every division inside an organization (except for IT), marketing is the most fluid, dynamic, and ever-changing and requires a constant reinvention of your skills and knowledge. The ability to stay relevant and fresh with every new technology disruption, challenge from your competition (which changes frequently), maturation of your buyers and users, and new go-to-market approaches, is fatiguing and crippling to many marketers—often without them even knowing it. Long-term sustainability in a marketing role requires a nimbleness of thinking, and an enormous level of self-awareness few of us actually have. I'm not suggesting you throw in the towel every time the landscape changes. Hardly. What I am suggesting is that *you* own deciding when *your* gig is up. Don't leave that to someone else. I once heard a both wise and offensive axiom, which is: "You're likely never in the room when your future career is being decided." Ponder on that for a moment, and your self-awareness and propensity for self-disruption should immediately increase.

Disrupting yourself doesn't mean you're put out to pasture to graze. Look at me—I left the CMO role and now I'm writing books, speaking, consulting, advising, and coaching. And frankly, I'm having a blast and making the most fulfilling contribution of my career. It takes a level of fearlessness that I'm not recommending everyone execute on immediately after reading this challenge. Be thoughtful. Be more self-aware. Be real with yourself. Ask, "Is what got me here going to take me there?" I implore you to become more mindful of when the demands of your marketing role have eclipsed your own talent, and determine your fate by deciding on your own when it's time to move on, move over, move up, or move out. All of which I've done.

In the words of Whitney Johnson, "Disrupt yourself before you're disrupted." I've also heard it expressed as "Act or be acted upon." Keep your ears to the ground, read the tea leaves, or even better, just ask. Ask your leader how long they think you should stay in your marketing role and use that as a reminder of when you may be peaking and it's time to move on. Because in marketing, your role is always on the chopping block. So pick up the axe and be prepared to swing it yourself.

FROM MESS TO SUCCESS:

DECIDE YOUR OWN TENURE

- Consider registering for FranklinCovey's *On Leadership* podcast. I promise you it will add significant value to your life—personally and professionally. Google "On Leadership with Scott Miller" and subscribe today or visit FranklinCovey.com.

- Think carefully about what you'd like to accomplish through your marketing contribution:

  - Can you achieve it in eighteen months? thirty-six months?

  - Are you building a clear plan to execute on the goals you've committed to so you can declare victory and move on to something greater?

  - Remember Acuff's advice: "Perfection is the enemy of completion."

- A wise coach of mine said to me once, "There comes a time in everyone's career when you've given 90 percent of what you have to offer your employer and you've also taken from them 90 percent of what they have to offer you; and the last 10 percent, either way, may not be worth the effort."

  - What's your percent?

  - Given your percent, what is your next step?

- Assess where you are on your career track:

  - Have you discussed with your leader what's next? Or is that conversation premature or too awkward or too scary, so you're avoiding it?

  - Accept that there is likely some dissonance going on between how you and your leader see your career. Take control of the dialogue by showing the courage and vulnerability to ask for their assessment, in real time, of your skills, contribution, and expected tenure. *Nobody has these conversations with their boss, which is why everyone is caught off guard during a difficult performance appraisal—or worse, when they're terminated.*

- Take control of your career so that you decide when it's time to make a move. The more you understand your reality, the more you can accomplish your goals and be in control of your destiny.

CHALLENGE 7

BRUISE HARD AND HEAL FAST

Do you wallow in pity, or can you pivot in real time?

As the former leader of marketing for a public company, I am well acquainted with the need to drive profitable growth and meet financial commitments. I also appreciate they must happen concurrently with providing solutions that drive your client's success *and* while developing a culture where associates chose to stay engaged. To quote FranklinCovey's CEO, Bob Whitman, our company is designed to be a "workplace of choice for achievers with heart." A great goal!

As a member of the executive team, I had responsibility for more than marketing and business development. I led the public relations strategy, multimillion-dollar licensing partnerships, books and media business, and a business channel with over 150,000 clients certified worldwide who teach our solutions inside their employing organizations. This channel was significant for us from the start, both in terms of margin and velocity, but also for nurturing our thousands of brand ambassadors around the world. These professionals, often in human resources, leadership, diversity and inclusion, or organizational-development roles, were vital to our business and championed us every time they moved and joined a new organization.

I cannot overstate the role FranklinCovey's client facilitators played in our international growth and furthering our mission to build great leaders inside great organizations. They represent significant revenue and incalculable worth to our brand equity and expansion. Tell me you don't wish your company had, at any given time, thousands of clients using and enthusiastically evangelizing your services.

For many years, I was responsible for keeping this channel active, engaged, and evergreen. On average, we certified about five thousand new client facilitators each year with the goal to keep them enthused and ordering participant materials. We focused on building their business acumen and ability to connect our solutions to their business needs, refining their classroom teaching skills, perfecting their content knowledge, and enhancing their marketing skills so more divisions inside their companies would "hire them" to train our solutions. An important caveat: none of these clients worked for FranklinCovey or were compensated by us for their roles. As part of their own job responsibilities, they became certified facilitators and benefited greatly from that credential and being associated with our brand. It's a great mutually beneficial relationship. This is not unlike working at General Motors, earning the Six Sigma or Lean-certified credential through specialized training with an outside vendor, then training others inside GM as part of your role.

We became quite adept at serving these in-house facilitators with different campaigns, and our team churned out some of the best initiatives to support their training needs I've ever seen in the industry—support videos, books, tip guides, webcasts, discounts, and offers that were wildly creative and attention getting. A major goal was to cross-certify current facilitators into multiple curriculum areas so they could bring greater value to their organizations and be in a position to purchase more participant materials across varied solutions.

I've shared this extensive background to set up the point of the chapter: Marketing was Midas.

We became so adept at the quarterly campaign that it turned into a bankable strategy, good for every stakeholder. But like the story of Midas, our hubris (i.e., "mess") nearly got the best of us. It all started when I pitched the CEO on an initiative that included a pack of three-by-four-foot posters with author quotes and pithy insights drawn from our own content to reinforce our solutions inside our client's buildings. The clients would love these beautiful posters and hang them in their lobbies and in their conference and training rooms. They get great art; we get great brand reinforcement. Masterful. Pure marketing genius (thank you very much). More posters meant more training, which improved their results, which sold more training materials, which drove more profit and gave us the opportunity to expand our mission.

The CEO, pleased with our track record of balancing what our clients valued with revenue generation, green-lit the poster idea and budget. Our team set to work designing said posters for a massive direct-mail campaign to over five thousand valued facilitators. After about ten days of serious contemplation, design, editing, and robust debates (including a supply-chain argument about mailing posters without damaging them), we triumphantly spread the finished artwork on the boardroom table and summoned the boss. Stepping back to allow the CEO to admire our unparalleled creativity and marketing prowess, we were certain we'd hit the bull's-eye once again. It was going to be epic.

What was epic, however, was how underwhelmed he was.

Not one prone to outbursts (he's likely the most emotionally regulated human I've ever met), the CEO scanned the posters and calmly said, "I don't think this is it." He then offered some pointed advice and suggested I go back to the drawing board.

At this point, I had two options: Lose my cool and unload on him (making sure to reference his bewildering small-mindedness, lack of vision, and lack of appreciation for how hard the team had worked the last two weeks), or, with an uncharacteristic amount of restraint, ask a few clarifying questions and then return to my team, hat in hand, and share that our Midas touch had come to an end. This was going to be a blow.

And it was.

The team had worked tirelessly on the project and felt it was just as praiseworthy as all the previous marketing masterpieces. And truth be told, I agreed. But a key stakeholder was our CEO (duh), so my job now was to pivot—as in turn on a dime and create something new that would exactly match the CEO's vision. I don't know about you, but most of us can't predict what our CEOs want, even if we had a divining rod at our disposal. Thankfully, my CEO will find this quite funny when he reads it. Yes, that last line was some subtle conditioning. I'm not an idiot, people.

I had to check my ego by starting over. Completely over. To make matters worse, the posters needed to be printed without delay if the campaign was to deliver the financial results I'd signed up for. See a theme here? Marketing owned a clear revenue goal and the CEO expected us to deliver. Which we would... somehow. We'd spent our entire runway and there was no additional time to re-create the posters, so it had to be done insanely fast.

The rest is kind of blurry. We licked our wounds, used a few choice words to describe the situation (not the CEO; we're quite fond of him, actually), then created magic like never before. We dug deep into our creative reservoirs, and in forty-eight nonstop hours, summoned the CEO back for Round Two. Knowing we had felt just as good about Round One was a stark reminder that things could go sideways again. But the CEO was elated, and we'd scored another win.

The campaign was a massive success with our clients, and we'd once again met (and exceeded) our commitment. The lesson: bruise hard and heal fast. Had I argued with the CEO or tried to convince him of our hidden genius, it would have diminished my credibility and instilled a mindset that I was rigid in my own opinions and incapable of taking feedback—an arrogant partner focused on what *I* wanted. My potential marketing mess ironically came from my past successes: I'd been conditioned to win through an undefeated marketing streak. Up until the point I lost, which we all do eventually. Fortunately, I allowed myself to bruise hard. Yes, it's painful, so give it a moment, take a breath, then move on and get back to work. In the end, my team and I gained more credibility by returning to our war room and cranking out a whole new set of proofs than had I tried to win the CEO over with the first set of posters. This would have been the classic shortsightedness known as *winning the battle but losing the war.* Here's a keen insight, so check in: I had watched too many otherwise talented leaders dig in on issues and win them in the short term, but lose the confidence and even the respect of the CEO in the long term, often because he found them inflexible, uncooperative, and even dogmatic. Pick your battles wisely; pick your wars even more so.

Another lesson is that every first idea isn't always going to work. Welcome to life and the constantly iterative world that is marketing. Even Ernest Hemmingway admitted, "The first draft of anything is shit." So unless you're a better wordsmith than Uncle Ernest, go ahead and check your ego. Resist stepping in a marketing mess by allowing yourself to bruise hard and heal fast. And become a nimble, humble partner willing to do whatever it takes to deliver on your commitments and change course midstream when necessary. I can assure you every CEO wishes their marketing teams operated this way. In the words of Dr. Stephen R. Covey, "Humble leaders are more concerned with what is right than being right."

FROM MESS TO SUCCESS:

BRUISE HARD AND HEAL FAST

- Assess how adept you are at bouncing back from adversity, feedback, or disappointment. (You'll likely rate yourself higher than a critic or detractor in your workplace would.)

  - Ask some colleagues to assess you on this competency. But don't just ask your best friend at work.

  - Include a colleague who worked on projects with you and may not be your biggest champion. This will require you to move outside your comfort zone, but it is an invaluable way to get unvarnished feedback.

- Set a goal to become nimbler, both emotionally and mentally.

  - Consider role-playing with a friend, spouse, or team member by having them "come at you" with reasons why your latest idea/plan/dream isn't viable, and build not just your resiliency, but your ability to create alternatives.

  - Recognize that most marketing initiatives are three steps forward, two steps back, so stay resilient until you land your best work.

  - Flex your thinking when necessary. Great marketing leaders are willing to change their mind.

- Have an emotional contingency plan.

  - Keep the big Plan A bets where appropriate, but always have a viable Plan B in the hopper to keep the momentum moving when you're forced to pivot and draw upon them.

  - A good contingency plan will capture an event's likelihood and impact (low, medium, and high), then present several mitigating strategies to employ if the emotional event takes place. Look online for more suggestions and examples of contingency planning you can draw from.

- Pull from the experience of event planners and others who have learned to be nimble. Every event planner I know or have worked with has an endless array of backup plans and options to pull from. I think they are some of the best hires an organization should consider, including on their marketing team. Take every opportunity to recruit and learn from such valuable team associates.

CHALLENGE 8

LOTS OF STUFF
WON'T WORK

*Are your contributions causing more
problems than creating solutions?*

One of my favorite, and certainly most recommended, business-leadership books is Liz Wiseman's *Multipliers: How the Best Leaders Make Everyone Smarter***.** This book has unequivocally had the largest impact on my personal leadership style.

Liz writes that as leaders of people, our job is not to be the genius in the room but rather the genius-maker of others. It takes a very secure, confident, and vulnerable person to live up to this standard. Liz also states that, although our goal is to be Multipliers of others, we all fall into becoming "Accidental Diminishers." The nine Diminisher profiles include Idea Guy, Rapid Responder, Strategist, Always On, Pacesetter, Protector, Rescuer, Optimist, and Perfectionist.

Reading the description of the Idea Guy stopped me dead in my tracks. "The Idea Guy is a creative, innovative thinker who loves an idea-rich environment. He is a veritable fountain of ideas that bubble up for him 24/7, so he bursts into the office brimming with new ideas to share with his colleagues."[3] I wrote about this in *Management Mess to Leadership Success*, but I'm going to revisit it here as it relates perfectly to this challenge.

A mess (weakness) I have is grounded in a success (strength). I'm a rather impulsive person, and as I've thought more deeply about it, I've come to realize much of my impulsivity and bias for action is grounded in my own creativity. I wasn't necessarily born extremely creative; it's more likely the result of a natural curiosity complemented with an insatiable desire to read. Since high school, I've read three print newspapers a day, subscribed to forty-two different magazines monthly, and polished off fifty-plus books a year. You can't help but learn a few things when you're spending that much time with your nose in the printed word.

Now combine my creativity with my impulsive nature and you can see why I'm the proverbial Idea Guy. At first blush, I would have assumed being an Idea Guy was an unparalleled strength in a marketing career.

---

3   p. 193-194 Wiseman, L. *Multipliers, Revised and Updated: How the Best Leaders Make Everyone Smarter.* New York: HarperCollins, (2017).

And in some ways, it is. But in others it definitely isn't. In my own case, I can serve as a fire hose of great ideas and, as a result, risk becoming a powerful distraction to the organization as it tries to narrow its focus and minimize its pursuits. In short, even our overdone successes can lead us into messes. A way out is to embrace the title of this challenge and recognize that lots of stuff won't work. But that mess isn't always solved with more inputs—meaning more ideas, more creativity, more options... You might think this is the resolution because marketing seems to some like a game of odds. This may sound intuitively true, but it's not. Marketing, like any other business practice, is best accomplished by narrowing the focus and becoming more disciplined: testing, retesting, challenging, inquiring, listening. You get it. That doesn't mean you shut off or shut down your creativity. It does, however, mean you recognize that more is not always better. Better is better (see Challenge 13).

"Lots of stuff won't work" is a marketing truth, and I'd like you to think carefully about your contribution to that reality. Is your own unbridled creativity, boundless energy, or (like me) your impulsivity contributing to your success or failure rate? If you were to slow down, think through your strategy more deliberately, resist moving straight to considering tactics, and benchmark your genius ideas against some other marketing professionals and success stories, might you improve your own hit rate?

The purpose of this challenge is to reinforce several points. Are you part of the problem and, if so, how can you reduce your negative contribution? I've found my own brand and success rate has improved when I employ some of the following disciplines.

- **Reduce my compunction to "save the day."** When I constantly try to be the hero, I do so by throwing as much proverbial pasta against the wall as is possible. Some ideas stick, while others don't.

- **Minimize or even eliminate a phrase I say way too often.** "What if we were to...?" This nearly always results in a new project for the marketing department and the perpetual, self-fulfilling cycle of stuff not working. It also leads me to distract otherwise competent leaders from becoming more focused on sound ideas that we're currently underexecuting.

- **Speak last.** I've spent too many meetings metaphorically "rushing to the front pew of the church" to claim the high ground and, as a consequence, unintentionally shaming everyone sitting behind me. Ever been in a meeting with me? I start offering solutions often before we've fully defined the challenge and determined what success even looks like. This is known as "a solution looking for a problem" or "moving too quickly off *what* and onto *how*." Solving *what* first is eminently more important than solving *how*. Candidly, solving *how* is easy, because it's all about tactics, and tactics are usually fun. *What* is your strategy and requires deliberate contemplation and rigorous challenging of your own assumptions. Less fun.

  Be cautious not to find yourself discussing tactics (*how*) when the topic at hand is still strategy (*what*). Stay with strategy as long as necessary, then move to tactics, where your best creative ideas can be better received because they're timed right. Your creative brainstorms may feel good at the time, but the fact is, you're likely not managing your brand well as you rush to a solution that ultimately may not work.

  It's not unusual for disciplined, competent business leaders to fall victim to the charisma and creative influence of the marketer in the room and for the campaign to eventually fall short of success because everyone was a bit caught up in the razzle-dazzle. This often happens because the marketer hasn't thoughtfully listened and aligned with the strategy. Be careful of your influence, power, and timing. It's likely more significant than you recognize.

- **Organize and compartmentalize your creative solutions.** Instead of overwhelming the team, committee, or meeting with every possible idea that comes to mind, I've improved my ability to silently determine if what I'm cooking up to impress the team is the right solution for the problem we're discussing. While Idea X may be your penultimate creative solution, it might best be deployed to Problem Z instead. And for that matter, Problem Z hasn't even surfaced yet in conversation and likely won't for a few more months. It may be the wrong meeting with the wrong people discussing a different problem.

I'm going to be especially vulnerable now and share a significant mess that trailed me throughout my marketing career. I work with a lot of smart executives. Many have MBAs from Ivy League schools, and almost all of them are older and more seasoned than I am. And every one of them is clearly more emotionally mature, deliberate, and measured than I'll ever hope to be. That's *their* smart. *My* smart is my creativity. With no humility, I am an exceptionally creative person. So in order for me to feel "smart" during the strategy (*what*) part of a conversation, I almost always move too quickly to tactics (*how*) because that's where my validation comes from. It makes me, perhaps pitifully, feel like an equal at the table. As a result, I've consistently been seen as the guy trying to solve a problem that hasn't yet been fully vetted. I'll be candid, it's hurt my brand. Not irreparably—the team I work with is quite endeared by my good intent, and they value the "smart" I do bring to the table—but not every culture has the same standard, so what may work in my current organization may never work in yours.

Simply put, I bring it too soon.

I'm always better off resisting my urge to talk and staying calm, being quiet, listening more, and waiting for the opportunity—which is always later than I think—to share my creative idea. In the immortal words of Abraham Lincoln, "Better to be thought a fool than to open your mouth and remove all doubt." Few will judge you poorly for being a great listener.

Another challenge to reinforce is, despite how deliberate you've become, some stuff just ain't gonna work due to factors outside of your control, and you need to be mentally and emotionally prepared for that eventuality. You've just read about "Bruise Hard and Heal Fast" in Challenge 7, so you're well on your way.

When you expect that some stuff will fail, that doesn't mean you don't give it your all to turn around any missteps; but when it's truly unrecoverable and your marketing campaign falls short of expectations, what's your process for a postmortem? One of the most valuable marketing tools I've learned is the postmortem. After every campaign, large-scale conference, product or book launch, or multicity tour, our team is fiercely dedicated to the debrief where we all check our egos and talk openly and freely about what worked and, more importantly, what clearly didn't.

This postmortem debrief is crucial to prevent any repeats. Illustrated below is a list of points our team typically investigates, regardless of the results.

- **Review the original goals.** Were they anchored in reality, or instead wildly, ridiculously ambitious? Stretch goals are vital for growth both in revenue and in our team's skills, but goals so aspirational that you can't accomplish them can crush you and your team's spirits and stifle momentum. Be careful to set goals that, when accomplished, build trust and confidence while teaching valuable lessons that add to your future capabilities. Were your goals crafted such that you measured success throughout and could have known sooner that things were off track? What success and failure indicators where built into the initiative to scoreboard and debrief in real time? As the marketing leader, have you created a culture where it's safe and people are encouraged to raise concerns early enough to address them—especially if it's your (the boss's) idea that needs challenging midway through. Every leader, regardless of organizational level, should have a copy of Hans Christian Andersen's *The Emperor's New Clothes* sitting open on their desktop for ready reference and reflection. Not familiar with the book? Trust me—go buy it!

- **Consider the wins and losses.** All successes and failures have both. A marketing campaign that fell short of revenue expectations might still contain invaluable lessons that can be applied in the future. I don't scrape and dig if wins and losses aren't apparent, but acknowledging our messes, more so than our successes, is where we grow as professionals. My leadership style is high on courage, and therefore we discuss every point that went well and dig deep into the *why* behind those that didn't. If you want to achieve exponential growth in your own skills and those of your team, allow no sacred cows. Begin with your own contribution; when you own your mess, you make it safe for others to own theirs. If, as the leader, you're both confident and vulnerable enough to tear into your own ideas and contribution first, then you create an environment for others to do the same with their own.

- **Find out whether team members were aligned to the right tasks.** Newsflash: Process is not my strong suit. I've never had a natural linear thought in my entire human existence. I've had to work deliberately to develop this skill, and even at fifty-two, it's still a competency I struggle with. Although well-intentioned, I've often haphazardly assigned tasks to members of the team without considering their natural talents or role alignment. To this point, I've become increasingly willing to share big ideas and plans with the team and then step aside, sometimes even physically out of the room, and let them decide who owns what and report back their decisions to me. It's worked well with a team of high-trust, highly talented members. I've carefully hired people with strong maturity and self-awareness, so they're very capable of stepping up and complementing my own messes. In most cases, they know best who should own what. To this point, when we now hold multihour strategy meetings on a new initiative, the entire team develops the agenda and purposely excludes me from set parts of the meeting so I

MARKETING MESS TO BRAND SUCCESS

don't mess it up. Offended? Not in the least. Many of their talents are in fact better unleashed without me commenting on or stifling every idea I hear. Candidly, with my absence comes greater efficiencies and team involvement—increasing the odds of what can and will work. I'm not saying I've gone on sabbatical or my salary is unnecessary. It's quite the opposite.

Secure and self-aware leaders know when they're not needed and, more bluntly, not wanted.

Sometimes the "stuff" that isn't working is because the leader is present and isn't adding value or is disrupting, diminishing, or suppressing conversation. Although well-meaning, sometimes the team just needs the leader to get out of the way. Surprise! Sometimes that leader is in fact *you*.

At the right time, I'm then invited to review the collective plan and add my own expertise where needed. When you can get to this point in your career, which took me decades longer than it should have, you've moved from a marketing mess to brand success.

- **Don't guess at metrics regarding budget, timelines, or delivery dates.** One of my favorite questions to ask when someone states what appears to be a fact is, "How do we know that?" A colleague might state in a planning meeting that "all the materials have arrived." I'll respond with, "How do you/we know that?" Frequently, they will say, "Because I tracked the shipment and it's been delivered." Can I tell you how many hundreds of times I've been told "the materials have been delivered," only to discover that only three of five boxes showed up? Or the boxes were delivered, but they weren't *our* boxes. Or our boxes did in fact arrive, but only 150 kits were in them, not the 190 we needed for the conference.

You get the point. There's a fine line between micromanaging and setting a high quality standard. Develop a strong sniffer to root out those who are guessing. I always want the facts, not your best hunch. Guessing, even on small items, leads to guessing on big items. I also clearly state with my team, "I am pushing on you not because I don't trust you; I am pushing on you because I want to tighten your skills and accuracy and reduce conflict and messes by staying on the same page throughout."

- **Allow every team member to challenge decisions and outcomes.** The safer the culture, the more willing everyone is to speak up. When, as the marketing leader, you set the tone with your team that no topic is off limits, you are never lied to. And lying, although often well-intended, always ends up screwing you. Your team members (or for that matter, everyone in your life, including your spouse/partner, children, and mirror) will lie to you in direct proportion to how safe you make it for them to tell you the truth. Do you blow up and lose your cool when someone tells you a shipment is late? No dummy would touch that stove burner twice. Welcome to the lying culture *you* have built. When you, as the marketing team leader, aren't getting accurate information, or team members don't speak freely during the postmortem, this is 100 percent your fault, responsibility, and imperative to correct.

How much of the stuff that's not working could work in the future by implementing any of the insights shared in this challenge?

FROM MESS TO SUCCESS:

LOTS OF STUFF WON'T WORK

In addition to the many tactics and potential actions outlined in this chapter, here are some important planning actions you can take:

- Recognize that everyone has blind spots—even you and me.

  - Privately, with nobody watching or judging you, make a T-chart (a simple listing of "pros and cons") on a sheet of paper and write a theme such as "My Strengths" and "My Weaknesses," or "How I Focus Others" and "How I Distract Others," or even "How I Add" and "How I Subtract."

  - Use whichever heading will tighten your thinking on how you are part of the solution or problem regarding what's working and what's not.

- Open your calendar and set aside time for uninterrupted thinking, perhaps at the start of each day or even the beginning of the week.

  - To quote Nir Eyal, author of the bestselling book *Indistractable*, "People prefer doing to thinking."[4] Remember, *how* is doing; *what* is thinking. You may have to get out of your comfort zone as you begin to build muscle memory in this practice. And to further quote FranklinCovey's chairman and CEO, Bob Whitman, "Thinking is a legitimate business activity."

  - Use your T-chart to consider what you should start, stop, continue, or fix. Have the courage to let go of things you might enjoy, but that just aren't working.

---

4   p. 76 Eyal, Nir. *Indistractable: How to Control Your Attention and Choose Your Life.* London: Bloomsbury. 2019.

Take a blank T-chart to a colleague (or your spouse) and have them complete it with you in mind so you can review it later. This will probably take an extra dose of courage on your part (liquid or otherwise).

CHALLENGE 9

DON'T ONLY DO WHAT YOU KNOW AND LIKE BEST

Are your passions and talents clouding what's actually best for the business?

I once read a statistic about how extraordinarily rare it is for people (less than 1 percent) to have a truly original thought during their lifetime. A bit insulting and depressing when you think about it, but as sobering as the declaration is, it's likely true. Knowing that there have been over a 110 billion thinking humans on earth, it becomes a bit less offensive. Let's fold our cards to this reality and take some refuge in the fact that many of us bring a different twist or angle to an established idea, invention, or business. Nothing wrong with that—many business unicorns build billion-dollar market capitalizations when someone, just like you and me, takes a unique twist on an idea and surpasses the originator.

Fifteen-plus years ago, I was living in Chicago and started a side hustle. I was single at the time and my Saturdays were my own. Come to think of it, so were my Sundays, early weekday mornings, and every weekday evening after six o'clock. And now that I've thoroughly depressed myself by recognizing my three sons have currently stolen all of my free time, let's continue.

One Saturday afternoon, after my decadent routine of eating breakfast out, reading *The New York Times,* hitting the gym, washing the car, taking a trip to the book store, and picking out the menu for my legendary Saturday evening dinner parties, I somehow tackled the pressing need to get a haircut, a massage, a manicure, or even a facial. Yep, I can feel your jealousy (or perhaps disgust) as you're reading this seemingly fictional paragraph. Then one day, I spotted a lady across the gym and, seven years later, found myself married and with three sons. My home now is like a nest of hungry baby birds, beaks open, all chanting, "529, 529, hey Papa, have you contributed to our 529?" Thoughts of well-funded dinner parties and relaxing massages have long since been replaced with college savings accounts (529s for the uninitiated) and a host of other parental responsibilities. But let's return for a moment to those carefree Saturdays in Chicago.

One day I was having my weekly (very manly) manicure at a local salon, and the manicurist whom I'd come to know after a few dozen appointments was wearing a set of earrings made from Italian lira coins. For you youngsters, lira was the currency that predated the euro in Italy.

The earrings caught my attention because of my own love of travel and the creativity it took to turn old coins into something fashionable. Curious, I asked the manicurist about them, and she lit up. With a huge smile, she launched into an extemporaneous story about her travels to Italy and how her husband had the extra coins from their trip turned into earrings as a gift that year. It was palpable how much joy wearing these earrings brought her. What started out as another normal conversation ended up with her passion becoming the spark for a thriving, entrepreneurial business.

I left the salon and within a few hours had launched a business: custom coin charm bracelets, my twist on her coin earrings. And like with all things in life, I went all in. I bought coins by the pound and dedicated dozens of filing cabinets to various countries and their numerous (seemingly endless) currencies. I organized and sorted them by size, color, and country, and soon I catered to women all over Chicago. Buyers completed a form with the countries they wanted on their bracelets, and I went to work shining and carefully placing coins in small sterling-silver, custom-size bezels. Coin charm bracelets were plentiful, but one customized to your own travels or heritage, to the best of my research, were not. In fact, they didn't exist.

The business exploded, and you could find my bracelets in mall kiosks, cruise-line gift shops, hair salons, and clothing stores. I came home from my corporate job to fifteen to thirty orders every night. Many evenings I worked six to eight hours until three in the morning, fulfilling all the orders. My growing business was validating and invigorating—I had truly created something from nothing and, honestly, it was one of the best feelings in my life. I had found a way to put a new twist on someone else's creative idea. Soon I was traveling to international jewelry shows, attending coin and numismatic conferences, and practically became a currency trader, as I needed to source my coins at the lowest costs possible.

After so many years in the training and consulting industry, I can't describe the level of pride that came from producing something *tangible*. I found instant gratification in seeing each finished bracelet match the checklist on a customer's form. The finished products averaged around eight coins and retailed for about $170. Not a bad gig, considering the potential sales volume. But it was also a one-man operation and I was that one man. I owned sourcing, logistics, production, packaging, marketing, designing, selling, fulfilling, delivery, invoicing, shipping, and multiple other business processes.

In the end (and as you can probably guess), I couldn't keep up with the demand without jeopardizing my day job with FranklinCovey. I had fallen into a specific kind of marketing mess as well: I was gravitating toward those parts of the business I liked the most—mainly sitting at the kitchen counter in my loft, selecting the coins, manually making each bracelet, putting it in the box, tying the bow, and taking immense pride in delivering the finished product. I was haunted with the parts of the business I hated: calculating, collecting, and paying sales tax, and sourcing backup vendors when a component supplier would inevitably flake out. I also hated the need to constantly lower my cost of goods by sourcing coins of equal beauty but of lesser face value when customers looking for a coin from, let's say, the UK wanted the $1.80 pound and not the much cheaper pence (which was killing my margin).

By doing what I knew and liked best, I neglected the many parts of the business I found boring, fatiguing, or beyond my natural skillset. But the very components I was avoiding were those that would have driven the sustainable growth necessary to scale beyond my local retailers. I dove deep into the areas I had expertise in or, truthfully, felt most validated by. I don't think I'm unique among most "solopreneurs," or for that matter, entrepreneurs trying to launch their own ideas and gravitating toward the parts they love the most. Looking back on it now, it likely would have imploded under my own desire to focus on what I enjoyed rather than what was vital to sustain and grow the business. I'll never know, because at exactly the time the business hit a tipping point, I started dating my now wife. Choices... she won, coins lost. What would you rather do at two in the morning—polish coins, or "hang out" with your new, super-hot girlfriend?

I don't think it's a stretch to say a similar tension and struggle exists for those of us with corporate marketing careers, or for that matter anyone who owns marketing in their business. Choice is so readily abundant in marketing that it can ruin the careers of the undisciplined and those with preset proclivities. The reason I think it's a unique challenge in marketing is this: How often is someone in finance or accounting struggling over whether to employ or not to employ a pivot table? I mean, come on! No offense to my pecuniary-minded colleagues, but I think it's reasonable to state that the options that exist in marketing divisions are multiplicative compared to other divisions with clearly defined charters and more focused options. Far too often, we're so focused on our strengths and personal passions that we allow them to cloud the types of marketing channels and mediums we employ that might be best for our business, industry, and potential customers.

For those of us who know and love print, we gravitate there. For the social media hounds, we lean there. Radio? Television? Direct mail? Billboards? Digital? Coupons? Promotions? Pop-up stores? Email and marketing automation? SEO? Animated videos? Fill in the blank. If we're truly honest with ourselves, we go where we feel safest, most knowledgeable, happiest, most fulfilled, and also most validated; and frankly, we market in the way *we* prefer to be marketed to. Which in reality may have zero correlation to the demographic and psychographic profile, or most vitally, the circumstances, of our prospective clients. I'm simply calling out the reality we all face in our marketing careers. We need to be introspective and mature enough to realize when we're advocating, or worse, employing marketing tools that satisfy our own creative outlet, as opposed to what is best for the business and what will attract and retain the attention of our ideal customer. Challenge your entrenched mindsets about the specific needs of the overall business and have the courage to admit when you're leaning into your own, likely subconscious, preferences.

One way to help mitigate doing only what you like the best is by remembering the topic of the opening challenge, which is to stay maniacally focused on the customer, their needs, and your organization's unique ability to solve them. When you employ concepts such as the smallest viable market and an enduring sense of customer centricity, it will naturally focus your marketing efforts on the right communication vehicles. Once you intimately understand who your buyer is, where they live, hang out, learn, communicate, network, search, etc., it will become readily apparent which marketing channels should be leveraged to engage in conversation with them and earn their ongoing attention and trust. This may sound aspirational, but it's as practical and applicable as any concept in this book. Focus on your customer, and that gravitational force will dictate almost naturally how, where, and when you make your marketing investments and which channels best support them. Doing so is almost an inoculation against falling victim to your own channel preferences or mediums of choice.

Sometimes we allow our team to validate our own preferences and passions and pull us away from the customer. If you want to see confirmation bias at work, go to your standard marketing department where someone who's otherwise well educated and who understands the marketing choices at their disposal sees a really cool animated video that went viral, falls in love with it, pitches it charismatically to their peers (and for that matter, their superiors), and everyone thinks, *This is going to be the coolest thing ever!* The only thing that outpaces groupthink is its momentum. And when it has zero impact on your prospective customer—because the best way to communicate to them is *not* through an animated video—you see all kinds of excuses manufactured to make up for a disciplined lack of focus on the customer.

I challenge you to take a few moments right now and just review all the venues, channels, and mediums you prefer to be marketed through. Then perform a quick cross-reference to see how many of those are finding their way into your marketing strategies in your professional role. You may be surprised at how subconsciously you, and for that matter all of us in marketing, advocate for what we enjoy most. The more you acknowledge this reality, the better you can separate what you like to do from what you must do.

FROM MESS TO SUCCESS:

DON'T ONLY DO WHAT YOU KNOW AND LIKE BEST

- Determine the things you don't like to do and are avoiding.

  - Ask yourself which parts of your marketing role bring you "discomfort" and how many of them you are avoiding, neglecting, or outright abandoning.

  - Brainstorm what you can do to feel less uncomfortable so that you gravitate toward them, not away from them.

  - Look for ways to improve your skills in that area.

  - If appropriate, delegate it to a colleague you trust and have empowered.

  - Identify someone to coach you so your confidence grows and the pain associated with it lessens.

- Determine the things you like to do and are possibly overdoing.

  - Recognize that all people generally lean toward their strengths.

  - Evaluate if there are marketing areas you're leaning too aggressively toward that may be damaging your brand or underdelivering to your company.

  - Deliberately align your passions with what you are good at (or can become good at) and with what your organization and industry values. Be prepared to move outside your comfort zone to new technologies, channels, and mediums.

CHALLENGE 10

AUGMENT YOUR BUSINESS ACUMEN

Do you understand the "business" of your business?

Let's level-set for a moment. Every associate in every organization, regardless of their role and the organization's size or mission, needs to understand their employer's money-making model. Yes, that includes the right-brained marketing managers known for their creative tours de force. It doesn't matter if you're an entry-level marketing coordinator working for a multinational Fortune 500, the office manager who co-owns marketing for a small dentistry office, or the program manager in a nonprofit where you wear five different hats and need to understand how your organization makes money or raises it. Even if you work for a private company where the owner may choose not to share or disclose financial details beyond specific project budgets, the more you ask, and thus understand, the greater the knowledge you'll acquire of how to drive profitable business (and perhaps earn a raise or bonus in the process).

First, I recommend Ram Charan's book *What the CEO Wants You to Know,* a remarkably simple yet useful look into what the author calls the basic building blocks of business—the five parts everyone must understand: cash, margin, velocity, customers, and growth.[5] Ram is a global coach and advisor to CEOs and boards of directors. His work is profound, and his business wisdom is unparalleled.

Then, learn how to read a profit-and-loss statement (P&L) and appreciate the role of a balance sheet. Why? Because every organization is either in business to make a profit or provide a service. Some both. And each has a budget with a P&L.

I was thirty-one before I competently knew how to read a P&L. If you haven't yet invested the time in educating yourself, check in as I walk you through the main components. If you're already well steeped in this, consider using this chapter as a reference to teach the uninitiated on your team and help them build their business acumen. You might be surprised at how many highly educated and competent professionals were never exposed to corporate finance, and would greatly appreciate and benefit from a coaching session on the topic from someone they trust

---

5   p. 86 Charan, Ram. *What the CEO Wants You to Know: How Your Company Really Works.* New York: Random House, 2018.

and respect. Let's be honest. Many cultures don't reward vulnerability. Exposing one's own lack of business acumen is rarely encouraged, so this may be an opportunity for you to become a transition figure in someone else's career.

I never earned an MBA, worked in finance or accounting (that's laughable), or took any formal business classes in college beyond micro- and macroeconomics, both of which kicked my behind (of which there was little left after statistics). My path—which I suspect is the same for many in marketing—followed a liberal arts education. There was a big focus on communication, interpersonal and public relations, organizational development, advertising strategies, etc. Having only taken the compulsory math courses (which, thanks to extra credit, I was able to pass), I entered my early career largely ignorant about corporate finance. I am self-taught in most of my financial literacy, but I graduated with honors from the School of Better Figure It Out or Find a Different Career. (Just don't ask me to calculate net present value (NPV) or issue puts and calls on stocks.)

Accept this tutorial with the same spirit in which I offer it: abundance and complete respect for your own areas of expertise. If my descriptions and examples fall flat for you, there are countless videos you can Google (and please do so; you'll need more than a working knowledge of this so your marketing decisions are both business-relevant and financially sound). But every marketer wanting to avoid a potential mess needs to understand the nomenclature and the basics of corporate finance.

P&L stands for profit and loss. There are three main components to any P&L: revenue, expenses/expenditures, and profit (your bottom line). Pull a generic P&L from the web and take some time to better understand its format. For now, however, let's just highlight the main categories. To make this easy and instructive, let's assume we own a hot-dog stand. Most of the clever names are already taken (like Perfectly Frank, I Dream of Weenie, Mustard's Last Stand, and What's Up Dog), so I've named ours The Salty Dog. Now that the fun part is over, let's go over some basic P&L terms:

Revenue (Sales). The amount of top-line money (cash, credit, or otherwise) we take in during the day. *The cash in the box that's driven to the bank when you fold up the umbrella and hitch the stand to your truck.*

Cost of Goods Sold (Cost of Sales). This is pronounced COGs (like a cog in a wheel but with an added "s"). COGs are the expenses associated with making/producing our product. *This includes hot dogs, buns, all our condiments, canned soda, ice, cups, etc.—basically, our receipt from COSTCO the night before.*

Selling, General & Administration (SG&A) Expenses. These are the additional expenses necessary to run The Salty Dog. *It includes the rent we pay for our little corner of the lot, the hourly rate (or commission) we pay employees, the propane gas tank we refill each day to boil the water, and any other costs associated with operating our business that aren't tied directly to the cost of producing the product.*

Marketing and Advertising. Any and all expenses related to promoting the business and location. *Here we capture the cost of Facebook ads, advertising in the church bulletin, taping and running a local radio spot, and printing business cards and flyers to hand out in the neighborhood.*

Technology. We probably don't need a lot of technology for our hot-dog stand, but this is any equipment, networks, or other technical needs required to run the business. *This includes the cost of our company computer, office supplies, the credit card swiper, and phone.*

Interest Expense. Most businesses have secured funding in the form of institutional loans to provide operating capital. And with that loan comes interest. *Remember that loan from Grandpa Chuck for the food truck and giant inflatable hot dog? Grandpa Chuck wants his money paid back on time… and then some.*

Taxes. One half of the two constants in life. *The Salty Dog will collect and pay taxes of all sorts, including local sales tax, state and federal income tax, unemployment and Medicare tax, and anything else "the man" wants to legally extort from us.*

Net Income. We're well on our way to building a hot-dog empire. *Finally, the $3.12 left from the twelve-hour shift is a shining spot for our families*!

An organization's P&L is typically tracked over specific durations: months, quarters, and certainly their fiscal year (which may or may not be aligned with a calendar year). Each of the bolded categories have separate subcategories, so all the expenses are carefully delineated for purposes of tracking increases and decreases and allowing all involved to "analyze the P&L" for trends, areas of focus, better cost containment, and to make better investments for growth in the future.

Beyond building your financial literacy, you'll also want to build a curious mind about the organization's goals, challenges, competition, cash collection, expansion plans, etc. The more you can learn about the varied business components, the more holistic your thinking will be. I have no idea who said this, but it stuck in my head: "You can only think as deep as your vocabulary is broad." Even gaining just a cursory knowledge of your organization's financial vocabulary will help you avoid the mess of being business illiterate.

FROM MESS TO SUCCESS:

AUGMENT YOUR BUSINESS ACUMEN

- Make the language of the P&L second nature.

  - If you're adept at reading a P&L, then take this opportunity to gather your team or anyone in your life who could benefit and run them through the categories.

  - If you work for a public company, access and review your annual report.

  - If you're in a private organization or perhaps new in business and a P&L doesn't exist, find one on the web and use it as a model to learn and teach from. It doesn't really matter; just make the investment in helping others become better educated.

- Find an expert to help you.

  - If your head hurts at the thought of calculating EBIT or EBITDA, (earnings before interest, taxes, depreciation, and amortization), take two Advil and walk over to a friend in finance or accounting. I am 100 percent certain any member would be delighted to talk you through all the lines on the company P&L and bring you up to sufficient speed.

  - As soon as you're proficient in it, you can heed the action in the bullet above.

- Learn your company's money-making model.

  - Sit your team down or meet with a senior leader and talk about the most impactful levers of your business and how you can drive them.

CHALLENGE 11

DEFINE YOUR SMALLEST VIABLE MARKET

Are you looking at your market through a kaleidoscope or a microscope?

Recently I joined Seth Godin, the leadership and marketing sage, on a conference call where he graciously and abundantly provided some coaching to one of our clients. He referred to himself as an iconoclast (a person who attacks cherished beliefs or institutions). I smiled when he said this, as I'm a bit the same, but Seth does it with a level of aplomb and grace I could only dream of. Next to Dr. Stephen R. Covey and his FranklinCovey cofounder Hyrum Smith, I've learned the most in life from Seth Godin. I read and reread his books and daily blogs like some read the Bible. Take no offense, I own several well-worn Bibles; it's just not my go-to source for marketing advice. And Seth's books and eleven years of daily blog posts have been instrumental in my own career journey. In case you didn't catch that, for eleven years Seth has produced a daily blog and *has not missed a day. Ever.* Name me something you've done every day, nonstop, without missing a beat for eleven consecutive years (4,115 days and counting) outside of the bodily functions that keep you alive, and you too will build influence like Seth Godin. If you've not subscribed to Seth's daily blog, put down this book and opt in now. It will be the most valuable investment you've ever made in your professional life. SethGodin.com. You'll thank me!

Okay, welcome back. It's likely been a few hours, but I forgive you for reading forty of his recent and archived posts. I would have done the same. It's like discovering Malcolm Gladwell's early articles from *The New Yorker*—you lose yourself in them and then realize it's way past midnight. Like binging Netflix, only for smart people who still read. (I'm going to get some hate email for that one.)

Seth is a prolific author of books and recently produced a masterpiece titled *This Is Marketing: You Can't Be Seen Until You Learn to See.* Seth's book is very different from the one you're reading now, and I highly encourage you to read his as well. *This Is Marketing* and *Marketing Mess to Brand Success* complement each other nicely. In fact, I think Chapter Four of *This Is Marketing*, titled "The Smallest Viable Market," is the most valuable chapter ever authored about the topic of marketing— and the obvious inspiration for this challenge. It introduces a concept that I can't seem to shake, likely because I violate it so consistently. With his permission, I've lifted a passage here (but be certain to invest in your own copy):

> The relentless pursuit of mass will make you boring, because mass means average, it means the center of the curve, it requires you to offend no one and satisfy everyone. It will lead to compromises and generalizations. Begin instead with the smallest viable market. What's the minimum number of people you would need to influence to make it worth the effort?
>
> If you could change only thirty people, or three thousand people, you'd want to be choosy about which people. If you were limited in scale, you'd focus your energy on the makeup of the market instead.
>
> The smallest viable market is the focus that, ironically and delightfully, leads to your growth.[6]

If you're like me, I start with the opposite—the largest viable market. It's much more intuitive. I'm incapable of thinking small. Friday night dinner party? Six couples, not two. Birthday party for one of the sons? Yes, please, I'll take six hundred balloons. Launch a new training solution? Bring on the 175-city global tour. My inability to think small is not always an asset (especially with a dishwasher that can't possibly hold dinner dishes for twelve people at eleven o'clock on a Friday night... after a few—okay, four—glasses of champagne).

I love the phrase "shock and awe," popularized during the 2003 invasion of Iraq (I have no comment on the legitimacy of that war—I just like the phrase). Shock and awe best describes everything I do. Cast your net large and imagine all the fish you'll scoop up.

---

6 Godin, Seth. *This Is Marketing: You Can't Be Seen Until You Learn to See.* New York: Penguin/Portfolio, 2018.

MARKETING MESS TO BRAND SUCCESS

Who among us is trained or encouraged to think small? Why waste your time starting so small and narrow? Life is short; go big. Defining your smallest viable market is so limiting. So restricting. So focused.

So genius.

When you invest the time to first carefully, even myopically, look at the profile of the person who should be buying your product, the odds that you'll get it right increase exponentially. Often, because we're so impulsive and many marketers and entrepreneurs/intrapreneurs have a bias toward action to grow and scale our business quickly, we lack the patience and discipline to implement Seth's advice.

The daughter of a friend of mine wanted to start a business selling boutique clothing online. His first reaction was to question the entire enterprise, given the implausibility of stepping out from the shadow of Amazon (and a host of other retailers) and finding a viable market. But then he asked her to narrow her focus: who was the smallest set of customers she was passionate about serving? What group did she know so well that she had a unique window into their clothing-buying preferences and challenges? As my friend continued to ask questions, they came to a surprising insight: his daughter had recently undergone bariatric weight-loss surgery and had been involved in several online communities dedicated to those who also had experienced the procedure. One of the personal challenges she and others faced was the need to buy new clothes (sometimes every couple of weeks) as the weight came off and the clothes no longer fit. Sure, there were plenty of online clothing vendors happy to keep selling smaller versions of their outfits, but there wasn't a vendor who spoke to this particular community and intimately understood both the challenges and rewards of being on such a journey. My friend's daughter began building a business model, recognizing that multiple purchases of the same outfits were likely. So she created support and discount structures that *increased* as her customer's sizes *decreased* (ultimately landing on a lifetime discount). When she focused on her smallest viable market, the path to serving her clients in a unique and empowering way suddenly became clearer as she literally started to list names of people, in sequential order, who might buy her product. Now, at first blush, you might be thinking that this is no way to scale. But the point is, getting obsessively focused on who is the first, second, and third person to become your customer, follow your blog, or subscribe to your newsletter. When this is the lens through which you see your market, you become obsessively focused on the desires, preferences, needs, profiles, etc., of those who are passionate about your product or service so you can deliberately and methodically expand that to further look-alikes. I wish her well and would encourage her to read Challenge 9 ("Don't Do What You Know and Like Best") so that her business doesn't end up like my coin charm-bracelet enterprise.

Sometimes the smallest viable market is discovered accidentally and perhaps later than desired. I recently watched an interview with Nancy Dussault Smith, former VP of marketing communications at iRobot, the company that manufactures and sells a very popular battery-operated, self-propelled vacuum—the Roomba. Initially named CyberSuck (seriously?), they never imagined their early adopters would be the elderly with heart conditions. To their surprise, initial buyers were heart patients who, due to post-surgery home confinement, liked to entertain often and thus kept their homes well vacuumed. Apparently vacuuming is actively discouraged for this type of patient because of the physical exertion involved. (These people must have had really heavy vacuums and exceptionally thick shag carpets, but I digress.)

iRobot learned of this particular viable market because they started receiving an unusual number of complaints about mechanical failures far beyond anything uncovered during the company's quality testing. Through further discovery and interviews with owners and users, they discerned that a wildly disproportionate number of early Roomba sales were purchased by or for heart patients, and because many of them were homebound (at least for a period of time), they were running their vacuums far more often than the typical homeowner. On average, the Roomba was being used four times a week—much more frequently than expected. Further, in some ways the vacuum was a companion, and more than 65 percent of owners named them (my mom named hers Betty).

These owners were both a bit bored and fascinated with the novelty of a self-directed robot vacuum and were literally running them into the ground.[7]

The story of the Roomba has great value for all of us. It's as much a lesson in understanding buyer personas (Challenge 20) as it is in defining your smallest viable market early on. I find it hard to believe that the market of heart patients would have been their self-determined smallest viable market, but who knows? Had it been, Roomba might have advocated for it to become "doctor-recommended" upon discharge and then their marketing might have been aimed at adult children feeling concerned about their parent's convalescence and social life.

Have you exercised the necessary deliberation to determine your smallest viable market? Truly, who (beyond your mother) is your first buyer? And once they've purchased, ask who's your second buyer? and third? And so on, one by one until you've nailed this trajectory.

It takes extraordinary discipline and patience to carefully and deliberately build up from your smallest viable market instead of falling back from the largest. This doesn't mean you can't exercise vision and huge stretch goals. You should see my vision board for this book. I started out with dozens of reader profiles I'm writing to: CMOs, VPs of marketing, marketing directors, managers, coordinators, product line leaders, brand managers—anyone in a company who is somehow related to marketing, public relations, advertising, sales, social media, etc. Then add in all the college and university marketing professors… Millions I tell you! Millions!

But there was a mess inherent in that perspective. As I applied Seth's advice to this book, my proposed smallest viable market became the person who was recently promoted to a new marketing role. I did a search on LinkedIn and found, well, let's just say plenty! So I sorted them and pointed my proverbial bat at the ones who actually earned a marketing degree as they were, in my estimation, the most likely to

---

7   Chris Savage, interview with Nancy Dussault Smith, Bandwagon, podcast video, https://wistia.com/series/brandwagon?wchannelid=u2joyabsw9&wmediaid=02mp0o52s5.

be serious about building a career in marketing. Of course, I think the overall viable market is larger, but this principle allowed me to focus on the needs and challenges of this person (knowing full well they would extend far beyond). Thus, you're not holding a college textbook on marketing practices. In fact, as you're discovering, I'm sharing very few of these academic insights as they have been written about exhaustingly by university professors. This is more a marketing-career manual—how to build your organization's brand and your own simultaneously so you create not just growth for your organization, but opportunities for yourself and those around you. I'm increasingly clear about the smallest viable market for this book, but that doesn't mean others—possibly you—won't benefit from the lessons I share, regardless of where you are in your sales or marketing journey. There's power in starting here: a focusing of your voice, a tightening of your logic, a heightened sense of empathy for the challenges that lay ahead for your smallest viable market.

I don't pretend to assume that these early career marketing professionals are 100 percent certain to buy this book (nor is that strategy alone sustainable for long-term, broad book sales). But it certainly focused my thinking on what I included in the chapters and their ultimate sequence, the curation of the particular messes and successes I shared, and whom I asked for an endorsement. It's a tempting marketing mess to start with the big. But it's often a surprising and ultimately rewarding experience to start small (and a great way to swap a marketing mess for a brand success).

FROM MESS TO SUCCESS:

DEFINE YOUR SMALLEST VIABLE MARKET

- Buy and read Seth Godin's book *This Is Marketing*.

- Resist your natural urges to plan, design, create, and communicate more rather than less.

  - Start slow and deliberate to achieve more in the long run. Think of the process of pouring washing fluid into your car's reservoir—do you use a funnel to focus the flow, or just dump it out all at once? Whether a manifold or marketing mess, the same principle applies.

- Start focused and small, and know your first customer, then your second, and then your third.

- Study the work of Rachel Hollis as a superb example of how to communicate to the smallest viable market. She is the author of numerous bestselling books including *Girl, Wash Your Face* and *Girl, Stop Apologizing*. In 2019, she sold more books than anyone in the United States, second only to former First Lady Michelle Obama. And when I say more, I mean 4.5 million books.

  - Pay attention to how Rachel speaks to her market's fears, pains, horrors, and dreams, and talks to millions of them like they're sitting at Starbuck's for their daily coffee after yoga. We recently met in her Austin office, and she referred automatically to her market as "she" and "her." This concept is so ingrained, it's second nature to her language. She obsessively uses the phrase "I'm in a relationship with *her*." And by "her," she means the millions of female readers, entrepreneurs, full-time mothers, and homemakers with a side hustle, etc., who look to her for advice, wisdom, and even relatability.

- Take a moment to follow Dave Hollis as well. He is the author of *Get Out of Your Own Way*, and applies the same principle with equal care, humor, and deliberation. I am a big fan of both Rachel's and Dave's writing and approach to their customers and followers.

CHALLENGE 12

INSTALL PROCESSES TO HARNESS CREATIVE MINDS

Is unbridled creativity driving or preventing results?

As with the other challenges in this book, this chapter is not a "how to" for installing and implementing marketing processes; there are plenty of experts and vendors standing ready to tackle that. Rather, this challenge is about the choice you will have to make, sooner or later, when it comes to them. A choice that, frankly, requires a good deal of introspection and may very well prompt you to disrupt yourself (refer back to Challenge 6: "Decide Your Own Tenure"). Or not. What's important is recognizing just how vital and likely inevitable this decision is going to be.

At the peak of my role as chief marketing officer, our team grew to about thirty-five associates. And for the first time in our team's history, we hired a senior associate from outside the firm. Like many companies, FranklinCovey has a strong "promote from within" culture, and very few senior positions are filled by external candidates. When they are, there's always a short honeymoon. Assimilating into our culture isn't easy for everyone, especially those working at our headquarters—a statement that can describe most organizations.

At the time of this new hire, our web strategy looked like the "Telephone" game. For those unfamiliar with how it's played, a story starts out one way and morphs into a completely different narrative than originally intended. Our website had dozens of separate sites, hundreds of landing pages, and thousands of individual pages with a litany of broken or dead-end links. We have an entrepreneurial culture (which is awesome), but it can lead to some overempowerment. In this case, it sometimes seemed that anyone with a budget (which was every leader) could create a website, or microsite for their own division, initiative, solution, book, or personal pet project. During this time, it was also the Wild West days of dot-com domains. If you had a cousin who could code, they were hired to build your division's site (and often on the platform of their choice). Reminds me of the CIS, or the Commonwealth of Independent States. Remember the attempt to keep ten post-Soviet/ USSR countries all cobbled into one coalition with a single dream? Don't recall the CIS? Exactly! It was unsustainable.

Within such a backdrop I took a risk and found someone with extraordinary competency outside of the organization. He was a progressive thinker, well educated, internationally experienced, with strong UX (user interface) expertise, and outside of our fairly insular culture—a culture I believed could lend itself to groupthink. There was a substantial upside to this new hire. Privately, however, I did worry whether he could thrive in our company's forty-plus-year "promote from within" culture.

Keep in mind our team was adding about three new associates per year as we increased our influence and delivered results (revenue). And like any small team, trust and communication are often easier to build when you sit ten feet from each other, when you can shout updates or swivel your chair for a team meeting—for that matter, every moment of the day can be a team meeting because of your relationships and physical proximity. This was the case with us for about five years; ten associates all worked within feet of each other, had very high trust, and everyone sort of knew everything because it was hard not to (wearing Beats headphones or AirPods at your desk wasn't a thing yet). As a result, the team didn't really require a lot of (okay, any) formal processes. We were nimble, forgiving, great at communication, and generally a lean, mean, revenue-producing machine.

Until we weren't.

We exploded from ten to thirty associates, and pretty much all hell broke loose. We had no processes and only my command-and-control style to fill the gap. Most days (I'm told), it felt like living in a small and authoritarian Middle Eastern country: resource-rich but held tightly together by a strong-willed dictator (me) who doled out direction and resources as he saw fit. Everything worked, at least on the surface (Google "Tahrir Square" for a short history lesson).

The marketing division was at a significant crossroads. We were responsible for dozens of different projects—some outright competing with each other for budget, time, and attention—in desperate need of prioritization. I wouldn't call it a nightmare, as the chaos was the result of the growing confidence flowing from the CEO. But with seven teams within one, it was a rapidly growing mess, and we were lacking the processes to move to success.

In a noble attempt to bring some sanity to this collage, my new outside hire proposed we communicate and provide status updates via a shared software service. He'd worked in several organizations that had cross-functional teams and was a strong proponent of this type of system. The members of the team and I agreed to give it a try, which could centralize updates and better coordinate all the emails, texts, drive-by conversations, luncheon updates, and instant messages we were using with each other. But do not equate agreement with commitment (a solid lesson in life). Nobody really wanted to adopt a new process—none less than me—so although we all said *yes*, we really meant *no*.

We signed into the new software, gave it some effort to varying degrees, and then like any process or system where team members suspect the leader's own commitment is lacking, everyone began to abandon it in rapid succession. The truth is, I liked our habit of working without a formal communication process, best described as "*Scott has an idea and shouts, 'Hey team, can you all come in for a short meeting?'*" Then I imparted pearls of unparalleled wisdom and loosely assigned tasks (typically, to the wrong people). Creative chaos in action, and that was our culture. But culture isn't sustainable without processes that ensure everyone is working in sync and that information is shared consistently and accurately.

My personal marketing mess: I was leading a team of thirty like I was still leading three. Nostalgic but untenable. The fact of the matter is my mindset/paradigm was that we didn't need processes. I found it to be constrictive, linear, and time consuming to document and report items that could be better updated by walking around and just checking in with team members. Because, as the leader, I had never truly bought in to the new digital-communication process, but rather just gave it lip service. It was doomed from the beginning. I own this, lock, stock, and barrel. As I look back (and this may sound self-serving), I wasn't sold on the benefit to *me,* the leader. The benefits were more about the broader team and, thus, I felt it was a significant cramping of my style. I'm not particularly proud of this; I'm just candidly sharing and owning my mess. The entire division had adapted their style to meet mine, and although that might be assumed to be a compliment to me, it had likely just become the standard operating procedure for all work around my creative style—which was no longer sustainable with the larger team. You might say I had become the "hairball" and the team was doing their best to orbit it, but they were constantly getting sucked in. The fact of the matter is, I'm not sure my self-awareness was robust enough to realize how necessary systems had become to both keep the broader team engaged and simultaneously harness my own creative contributions.

It may not come as a surprise to you that, within a year, I chose to step away from the chief marketing officer role because I came to realize my team's needs (process among them) had exceeded my capacity. I'm most proud of that admission and that the "new hire" associate who desperately tried to implement processes was now better set up under my successor to thrive. Incidentally, this talented new hire left within a year of me stepping aside, so perhaps my communication style or resistance to systems wasn't the only issue after all.

I'd place myself to the far right on a litmus scale of creativity. If 1 on the far left was high linear/process/systems thinking and 10 on the far right was high creativity/verbal expression/vision, I'd be a 74. It can be a superb skill when balanced with a team that appreciates your contribution, but a handicap if you don't recognize its impact and install (and support) systems to keep the trains running on time.

As I reflect on this pivot point in the division, I've come to realize our team members were tired, running into each other like Keystone Cops, and were craving some processes—ones that their leader would actually support and follow. They also loved the high of creating and executing new initiatives, many of which were extraordinary and separated us from our competition. Through some deliberate introspection, I realized that my identity shouldn't be lessened or squelched because I wasn't drawn to the adoption and implementation of marketing processes. Rather, it was okay to surround myself with competent associates who thought and operated more systematically so that there would be less chaos and more order for a growing team.

A leader, especially in marketing, where creativity is the starting point of almost every endeavor, requires an open, transparent, and trustworthy culture where it's safe to talk about your messes and successes in order to thrive. The safer it is for your team to know *why* you lean toward or away from systems and processes, the better they can acclimatize to them when the time comes. When done right, installing and adopting processes can harness a team's natural creativity so they feel respected, informed, and empowered.

In my case, the need for the division to have systems eclipsed my need to ignore them. This was a turning point in my own career and likely for those I left behind. I now marvel at the processes and systems in place—they have improved the culture, productivity, and outcomes of this group of highly competent professionals, a fact that I'm neither embarrassed about nor ashamed of, given my exit. I'm proud of my decision to step aside and of their ability to step up. Your tenure in marketing will likely offer you the same crossroads. How will you respond?

Processes are vital, and I've come to better appreciate them as a parent and spouse comanaging a busy home. I liken it to (forgive the gender prejudice) when I get excited and "do" four loads of laundry—meaning I put clothes in the washer and move them to the dryer, and my wife comes home with three fighting sons and finds four loads of clean and dry but wrinkled laundry shoved into baskets, often with stains because I didn't check for "ChapStick in pockets." She thinks and says, "Thanks, Scott, but no thanks; that's not really helpful." That's because she has a process that actually works and she sticks to it; whereas I follow my impulses, and not only lose multiple ChapSticks, but destroy plenty of clothes in the process.

FROM MESS TO SUCCESS:

INSTALL PROCESSES TO HARNESS CREATIVE MINDS

When it comes to the role you should play in installing processes, there are three obvious choices:

- Lean into a natural proclivity toward systems implementation (or force yourself to evolve to that) and be the champion and model for the rest of the team to follow.

- Recruit or empower someone who can fill the champion/model role for the rest of the team. This requires you lend your executive support and compliance while hiding any lack of enthusiasm.

- Disrupt yourself by moving to a new role, company, or even career. If tethering your creative impulses to an unwieldy system or process is too much, find another outlet so you don't wake up every morning hating your job (and your team likely hating you).

Recognize that highly creative people often feel constricted by processes. That's a natural part of the creative world—welcome to marketing! Embrace this and acknowledge it by discussing it openly and transparently with your team members. Demonstrate vulnerability by showing the willingness to own your mess around any potential lack of systems or processes, and make it safe for others to offer suggestions, solutions, or work-arounds so everyone can bring their best to the team. By leading on this, you will become a model where other issues may well surface, thus increasing trust and transparency in your culture.

CHALLENGE 13

MORE IS NOT BETTER; BETTER IS BETTER

Are you trying to boil the ocean?

This is a challenge everyone faces throughout their career, regardless of what division, platform, role, or contribution you're making in your organization. I'd like you to be thinking throughout this challenge about where can you focus on *quality*, not *quantity*—and how that recalibrated focus can improve your own brand and deliver better marketing results.

One of my successes is that after nearly thirty years in the leadership-development and performance-improvement industry, I have fairly immediate recall of a trove of inspiring and witty phrases and adages. However, one of my messes is that I overuse them. The title of this challenge is at the top of the heap. I love it and will keep saying it for no other reason than to address my own mess with it.

As Dr. Stephen R. Covey, author of *The 7 Habits of Highly Effective People*, was fond of saying, "To know, but not to do, is not to know."[8] Like most wisdom I don't live, the "More is not better; better is better" aphorism haunts me.

Allow me to kick this dead horse one more time by saying that the marketing profession attracts creative, right-brain types. I know, that's a gross generalization; but as an equal-opportunity offender, I bet a majority of CPAs are linear, left-brain thinkers who see most issues as black and white. Ask Enron's investors how much they now value the role "creativity" played in their accounting and finance division. To support my supposition, I live in a world of grey—pushing boundaries, taking on sacred cows, piling on projects, and constantly disrupting my own roles and skills. If my colleagues and friends had to use one word to describe me, it would be indefatigable. And it wouldn't always be a compliment!

The temptation to become distracted has never been greater, and it's not lessening. Next week, next month, next year, you won't have fewer choices in any area of your life; you'll have more, professionally and personally. Netflix isn't going to have fewer shows next year, and your leader isn't going to pull back on the need for more growth. Choosing

---

8   p. 109 Covey, Stephen. *The 7 Habits of Highly Effective People Revised and Updated 30th Anniversary Edition.* New York: Simon & Schuster, 2020.   .

from among options is a growing leadership competency that each of us needs to build and master. Which means we need coping tactics and strategies to ensure that focus and discipline are key talents and not afterthoughts. Because we're all subject to the mess of distraction, we can better resist the temptation when we're aware of it and place boundaries and rules on it so we're not constantly bombarded by it. A great example is that I'm well known for telling the team not to tempt me with too many ideas or tangential comments in meetings because I've never met a rabbit hole I didn't love to go down. Even if it's a life/game/industry-changing "This will make us Powerball-rich" idea, think very carefully before you pitch it to me, as the odds are I'll jump on board. Do yourself a long-term favor and don't tempt me with short-term ideas.

This propensity to be easily distracted by new and shiny things convinced my parents I suffered from ADHD. I've never fully understood their evidence, as being easily distracted in algebra class didn't equate to an ADHD diagnosis. Being bored with tasks that didn't interest me was not itself worthy of clinical intervention. How do you explain the fact that I'd play tennis for five hours straight on Saturday or read entire books in one sitting? Besides, when in life have I ever used algebra? (If you tell me I use it unconsciously every time I throw a wad of paper across the room and into the garbage can, then you may be right—but I still don't care. Because I always miss anyway. See, I told you algebra was useless!)

Could someone also explain why a mandatory class in my high school was... wait for it... AVC, or "Americanism versus Communism"? Pardon me, I'm a patriotic dude—I vote in every election and love my country—but Americanism? Is that even a thing? Sounds like the efforts of a few rogue school board members. Sorry, I've gotten distracted and now I've digressed (ADHD? Hmm...). I've just proved, once again, how prone we all are to distraction. And when I say all, I mean me.

Let's get back to the challenge at hand. Think for a few moments about the following points. Circle your level of agreement on a scale of 1–10 where 1 = "I can't even relate to this idiotic suggestion and am putting your book down to read something useful like *Everyone Deserves a Great Manager* by Scott Miller, Todd Davis, and Victoria Roos Olsson" (yes, this is another book recommendation), and 10 = "Scott, you nailed it—this is my life!"

> My life is prone to interruption. Across all of my tech tools, projects, commitments, and relationships, I've set myself up, perhaps unwittingly, to bounce across messages, projects, and incoming updates from countless, well-intended people and sources.

1   2   3   4   5   6   7   8   9   10

> I've come to like my brand as a multitasker, but on reflection, I admit my results across the board are compromised because of "too much."

1   2   3   4   5   6   7   8   9   10

> I'm a naturally curious person. I have varied (seemingly endless) interests and like to cultivate them at any opportunity, even if it's just for a few moments here and there throughout my day.

1   2   3   4   5   6   7   8   9   10

> In life I have many roles. I wear multiple "hats" at work and at home. I am more than just a dad, a sister, an aunt, or a project manager.

1   2   3   4   5   6   7   8   9   10

> I recognize that subconsciously, I take in hundreds, if not thousands, of messages daily, and my ability to resist them sometimes seems pointless.

1   2   3   4   5   6   7   8   9   10

> I need more deliberate career and business goals, which would act as a defense against the "Incoming!" artillery barrage of distractions.

1   2   3   4   5   6   7   8   9   10

I subscribe to the adage in my life, "Have a plan, or become part of someone else's."

 1   2   3   4   5   6   7   8   9   10

Obviously, these questions aren't scientifically based. But I'll bet if you're at all like me, you're drowning in a deluge of options, and that reality is bringing diminished quality and returns to everything you're doing. I want to reinforce the point that we can easily spread our focus too thin across seemingly great opportunities, and instead of our quality on three of them being an A+, it drops all seven of them to a C. In an ubercompetitive world, regardless of your role or industry, quality results have never been more highly valued. So become more mindful and deliberate about delivering better on less.

This is especially true in marketing, because everything could, in fact, be considered a worthy possibility. Rarely has anyone in Human Resources or Legal ever said that. I could keep going, but you get the point. The alluring concept of "more" is omnipresent in our lives, and as I referenced before, it's not lessening. In my first book *Management Mess to Leadership Success*, I share another adage I think about often: "You'll never have enough, until you've defined how much is enough."[9] I think I always need more and it's why I've included this chapter.

One of my regrettable messes during my marketing career was my sustained and insatiable need to take on too much. Way too much. People throughout my career have marveled at my "capacity." Well, if you're willing to make your *job* your *life* and burn through relationships to land your latest commitment, then you too can win the "capacity" medal. (Please reserve a space in the church pew for the capacity medal at my funeral. It will probably take the place of a person… or sadly, many. In fact, just to be safe, better clear the entire aisle.)

---

9   p. 113 Miller, Scott. *Management Mess to Leadership Success: 30 Challenges to Become the Leader You Would Follow.* Miami: Mango, 2019.

Here's a wakeup call whether you're in marketing, sales, product development, or something else. *More is not better; better is better.* This may seem counterintuitive, but if you're a realtor, more listings are not always better. If you're in sales, more six-figure opportunities in your pipeline are not always better. If you're a budding entrepreneur, more side hustles are not always better. More spouses are certainly not better (unless you live in certain neighborhoods in Southern Utah; and just so you know, the feds are looking for you, but the state not so much).

How do you avoid this marketing mess? Narrow your focus. Take some time, ideally away from your office, team, family, and the pressures of life, and decide what your contribution and legacy will be. What are you going to say yes to and, just as importantly, what are you going to (in a moment of extraordinary courage) say no to? Frankly, I don't do this enough. Like you, I have what often feels like insane and crushing obligations from my many life roles: father, husband, son, brother, uncle, brother-in-law, friend, neighbor, coach, author, executive, divisional leader, contributor, volunteer, podcast host, columnist, church teacher... it's endless. The longer the list, the more valued I feel. But I wonder why? What's missing in my life that I feel the need to take on so much? Why am I so insecure? Why do I feel the need to endlessly please my own leader to the point that I am willing to crush my team with insane amounts of work and am incapable of ever saying no? Does it really help my self-esteem, self-confidence, or self-worth? Honestly, I'm not sure. Better to close on your listing in sixty days and reap a stellar referral than to have twelve listings, most of which linger on the market because your bandwidth to stage, advertise, and show them is compromised. I get the benefit of volume, and there's a need for it, especially when you're in a commissioned sales role (first ten years of my career), but we can all benefit from better prioritizing all that volume.

In *Management Mess to Leadership Success: 30 Challenges to Become the Leader You Would Follow*, I was especially vulnerable about my career stumbles and insecurities. I wanted to author a different type of leadership book—one that was relatable and in which every chapter wasn't a success story (of the thirty challenges, I think I excelled at maybe three).

The book was so raw, in fact, that I shared dozens of examples where I'd either overcommitted and underdelivered or compromised my own quality because of my inability to focus, prioritize, or say no to projects that otherwise fed my ego, stature with my leader, or fueled the need to deploy my own creativity. Of the over two hundred radio and podcast episodes I've been interviewed for, the common opening of nearly every interview focuses on how surprised (and encouraged) the interviewer is that someone would invite such an honest and intimate peek at their professional career.

My response has typically been, "I don't think I'm that different from any other manager or leader; I've just come to know the power of vulnerability and 'owning my mess.'" One of my most obvious marketing messes is the tension my drive for quantity places on my unrelenting quest for quality. As you will learn in Challenge 30, "Set and Challenge Your Quality Standards," I'm obsessed with quality. It's my hallmark and legacy throughout my career. But because I'm equally obsessed with quantity, it has led to burnout, massive imbalance in my life, and a team working for and with me that's often pushed beyond reasonable limits, obviously resulting in compromised quality. Using an Olympic metaphor, I nearly always made it to the podium, but my national anthem wasn't featured frequently enough, as illustrated by a stack of bronze and silver medals when more could have been gold. Name the second-most-awarded swimmer in history after Michael Phelps. Right, you can't. I wish I had taken this favorite aphorism of mine to heart much earlier: *More is not better; better is better.*

I bet most of you are just as distracted as I am, without having to justify algebra lessons or blame anti-Communism indoctrination for taking up your time. Here's what's coming when you put this book down: A BARRAGE OF UNSOLICITED, CRAFTY, HYPERTARGETED MESSAGES AIMED AT HIJACKING YOUR ATTENTION IN EVERY WAKING MOMENT. If you think it's bad now, brace yourself.

Break free of this marketing mess by looking at all of your marketing initiatives and prioritizing them by which will drive the highest return, then exercise the courage to say no to the rest.

FROM MESS TO SUCCESS:

MORE IS NOT BETTER; BETTER IS BETTER

- Make a list of all the things that currently require your attention.

    - Rank and separate items into As, Bs, and Cs according to their importance.

    - Circle two or three that, if you were to eliminate them, the consequence would be negligible and the time and energy from which could be focused on something more impactful.

    - Set a goal over the next week to resist the temptation to take on the Bs and Cs (and as a result, your As will actually be executed upon).

- Learn to say no to the *good* that often comes at the expense of the *great*.

    - What will you do to help narrow your focus on quality over quantity? Consider enlisting the help of colleagues, mentors, or even your leader to determine the highest and best use of your time.

    - This may seem unrealistic in some cultures, but we all have blind spots, and sometimes a trusted colleague or leader—when extended the invitation to share insights into how you work, prioritize, and lead—can have a significant impact on your productivity and reputation.

- If your tendency is to say yes to everything, begin by saying no to yourself over small things:

    - No, I won't check my email or text until this report is complete.

- No, I won't call an impromptu team meeting to discuss my last genius flash of creativity until I land the campaign that's due this afternoon.

- No, I won't distract my team with any new ideas. Instead, let's execute flawlessly on what we've currently decided to do.

CHALLENGE 14

BE WILLING TO
CHANGE YOUR MIND

*Is your ego too fragile to allow you
to publicly change your mind?*

We've all worked for the marketing leader who was so intent on being liked (or who so lacked the courage to stake a claim or point of view) that they weren't known for holding any firm positions at all. It brings to mind a concept especially relevant to marketing roles because of all the inputs coming our way. And when I say "inputs," I mean suggestions, insights, opinions, comments, critiques, vitriol, feedback, data, analytics, A/B testing results, etc.—no matter how you dress it up, the barrage coming toward marketing is unrelenting. Thus, my challenge-requisite adage: "Stand for something, or fall for everything."

We've also reported to this marketing leader's alter ego (for some of us, it was the same person on the same day) who was so dogmatic and unilateral, that their position was unmovable. Even when presented with the most compelling data or real-time "This ain't working" evidence, these leaders remained stubbornly fixed in place. Instead of reflecting and opening a dialogue about third alternatives, they doubled down— usually because their ego was so fragile. Sometimes the doubling down does work though; just ask Bob Iger how unsupportive the Disney board was regarding the Pixar acquisition. In his book *Ride of a Lifetime: Lessons Learned from 15 Years as CEO of The Walt Disney Company*, Bob describes the rocky path regarding bringing Pixar into the Disney family. Had he not been so convinced of its strategic value and resisted the board's opposition, they would have lost Pixar, and Disney would be an entirely different company (not for the better) than the global media giant it is today.[10]

Then there's another type of marketing leader (which some of us have been)—the one who simply agrees with the last person they talked to. They've met with every team member, who have each expressed their position with varying levels of persuasion, confidence, charisma… and facts. And candidly, it wears the leader down to the point where the last marketing pitch they heard seems the most viable. This leader relents and announces the solution (to the chagrin of those who previously pitched).

---

10   p.119-120 Iger, Robert. *Ride of a Lifetime*: Lessons Learned from 15 Years as CEO of The Walt Disney Company. New York: Random House, 2019.

MARKETING MESS TO BRAND SUCCESS

In the whirlwind of marketing where opinions come fast and furious, this can be a dangerous leadership trait.

By now you know I love a good political corollary, so here's one for the offering: I imagine the most important role of the President of the United States is choosing their cabinet. In addition to leading their own massive agencies, these men and women serve as counselors and advisors on broader administration topics, or at least so one hopes. Read a few presidential biographies or watch the news and you'll see evidence of both groupthink and polarized positions so entrenched, they result in resignations, policy blunders, and prolonged stalemates—or worse, war. Many a president has been advised or coerced into a political position by an especially persuasive or charismatic advisor and lived to ultimately regret that decision.

A far cry from the Oval Office is the chairman's office at FranklinCovey. Members of the chairman's executive team have diverse functional roles, and we are required to advise and opine on weighty matters that affect acquisitions, expansion plans, product development, and often personnel issues that can all benefit from different perspectives. I took this role increasingly seriously the longer I was on the team, trying to take my own advice to talk less and listen more as I've learned how complex most issues are when raised to our level.

I came into the role of executive vice president of business development and chief marketing officer as a very confident, decisive, and deliberate leader. I suspect those traits helped me land the position, but as the topics became weightier with larger consequences, I found myself uncharacteristically less certain and clearly more contemplative. It became common for me to sit in three-plus-hour meetings with the executive team and have my position swing from one extreme to the other after listening to deep discussion and analysis from other very talented and experienced peers. But not always, as I sometimes became even more entrenched in my own point of view and worked diligently to win others to my side. Regardless, the objective was to find the best decision, and not validate preexisting ones.

As I look back, I don't know that I always served the CEO well, because clearly, like all of us, I had agendas (some hidden and others closer to the surface) and I wanted some credit for a winning argument. I shared in *Management Mess to Leadership Success* that the most valuable feedback I've ever received (and I've received a lot over the years) was from my CEO when one day he said in private after a team meeting, "Scott, you make too many declarative statements." I've reflected on this comment hundreds of times, and while it's made me no less opinionated, what I now *think* isn't always equated with what I *say*. I used to have a 1-to-1 ratio of *think* to *say*—now it's more like 10 to 1 (as in for every ten thoughts, I express one of them verbally).

The cost of always speaking your mind (or being overly declarative when you do) is that it entrenches your position and makes it harder to change your mind in those situations when you've "gone on record." I know of one very talented colleague whose communication style is a step beyond declarative to what might be called exclamatory. Everything this person says is "gospel," and because of their unilateral (you might even call it omniscient) style, they eventually roll back 80 percent of what they say. When more facts come out, a discussion is facilitated; or they're so backed into a corner, they realize how pitiful they look, and they end up reversing or making concessions on their line-in-the-sand position, consistently undermining their credibility. I'm fairly certain everyone knows someone like this (or will). Or worse, you might have just seen yourself in that previous description, which means you need to modify your style immediately.

I've applied this advice in my marketing career, mainly as I've aged, and uncovered the need to balance my instincts and experience with the ideas and backgrounds of those with more, or sometimes less, of both. My deeply entrenched beliefs about our customers, users, and buyers is challenged daily. The truth is, I don't look/act/think/buy as much like our customers as I think/hope/believe I do. How I like to be marketed to may hold no value for someone sitting to my right, as we may both consume the same products but for entirely different reasons (known as circumstance-based marketing).

A quick but vital segue: I teach a class in my church to ninth-graders (fourteen- to fifteen-year-olds), and I've discovered none of them have ever read a print newspaper or even held a print magazine in their hands. I have two of each in my briefcase as I write this (to their horror, I also still own and use a briefcase) and will buy several magazines and newspapers tomorrow, guaranteed! But with my students, like our customers, my preferences and perspective should never be assumed to be shared. Thus, the more we get locked into our mindsets, our belief systems, our paradigms—the way in which we see ourselves and the world—the more of a marketing mess we can find ourselves in. And the more we ground this mindset in verbal affirmations, the harder it is to dig ourselves out and adapt to a new reality. Tell me you've never stuck with a position you expressed verbally simply to save face. We've all done this, and it's a behavior we should be aware of and eliminate.

Remember that in marketing, as in life, there's a fine line between confidence and arrogance. You could fill an entire edition of *Harvard Business Review* with stories of CEOs who took a different (radical) path from what was advised and approved by their boards, and it resulted in wildly successful results for their shareholders and customers. Several more volumes could be filled with horrifying tales of belligerent leaders who were so blinded by their own hubris, that they drove the entire enterprise into the ground. Clayton Christensen and Karen Dillon, in their book *How Will You Measure Your Life*, report that 93 percent of all companies that ultimately achieved "financial success" had to abandon their original strategy because it was no longer viable, and instead pursue a new path that became increasingly apparent day by day. They refer to this as differentiating between deliberate and emergent strategies.[11] Or in more pedestrian terms, we might refer to it as being willing to change your mind. Think about this: 93 percent of companies who achieved "financial success" did so with a different strategy than the one they originally set out with (likely the strategy the CEO or founder was

---

11   p. 122 Christensen, Clayton, and Karen Dillon. *How Will Your Measure Your Life?* New York: Harper Business, 2012.

passionate about because it was their own idea). This proves the need for mental and emotional agility for leaders at all levels.

Here are some questions to reflect on:

- Look at your recent win/lose record. How many of the wins were *your* ideas? Does it even matter whose idea it was? In what cases does your ego—or the potential embarrassment that comes with abandoning a losing initiative—drive you to excessively defend or prolong a project or investment? Are you so personally attached to your own idea winning that you're willing to go down with the ship or make extraordinary excuses for why it's not "yet" working?

- What feedback mechanisms do you have in place with the field or your customers to ensure you know if your campaigns and messaging are working like you envisioned?

- How often do you look for evidence or interpret data to validate your own ideas and defend your belief that "in fact they *are* working when you look at it from *this* vantage point"? If you're digging too deep, that's in and of itself a sign to notice. Are you aware of the role that confirmation bias plays in your own decisions as you attempt to stick with a deliberate strategy when you might need to move closer to an emergent strategy? Conversely, are you willing to "place all your chips on red" when early and sustained evidence points to a marketing win, and consequently choose to starve or stop other campaigns to ensure funding and focus on a winning strategy?

Marketing often requires acts of courage. It rarely takes courage to shut down and close yourself off from both the opinions and data that present an alternative story. Instead, exercise the courage to listen more and talk less, and question more and declare less. Competent marketing leaders know when it's time to either throw in the towel and change strategies (or listen to the counsel of others suggesting the same) or go all in, if the evidence supports it.

Recently I had the privilege of interviewing former Hewlett Packard CEO and U.S. senate and presidential candidate Carly Fiorina for FranklinCovey's *On Leadership* series. An especially poignant story she shared took place during her campaign in the Republican presidential primary of 2016. After an especially poor showing in both the Iowa and New Hampshire primaries, her small team returned home to rest, recover, and reflect. The next day, there was an early-morning knock at Carly's front door: she knew it was Frank Sadler, her campaign manager, about to break the news that it was time to get out of the race. When Carly opened the door, to Frank's surprise, not only was she fully dressed—hair done, makeup on—she had a big smile on her face combined with a positive disposition. She announced, "Frank, I think it's time we drop out."[12]

Carly didn't share this story in a self-aggrandizing manner. Rather, she used it to illustrate that strong leaders must be nimble thinkers, have the robust ability to turn on a dime, bounce back from adversity and, perhaps more importantly, set those conditions where it's safe for every member of their team to do the same. Consider using Carly's example the next time you need to change your mind or be open to someone's challenging counsel on a marketing initiative you're heavily invested in. Carly may have beat her manager to the punch, but kudos to Frank as well for being willing to talk straight with his leader—someone who could have become the President of the United States. If Carly could abandon a run for the presidency after months of crisscrossing the nation and participating as the only female in her party in a series of nationally televised debates, certainly you can challenge your thinking on that marketing initiative you're so deep into.

---

12   p. 123 Miller, Scott. "Find Your Way: Carly Fiorina," *Franklin Covey On Leadership*. Podcast audio, January 7, 2020. https://resources.franklincovey.com/mkt-olv1/84-carly-fiorina

FROM MESS TO SUCCESS:

BE WILLING TO CHANGE YOUR MIND

- Inventory the last time you publicly changed your position on a campaign: Who should have led it? What should your own involvement have been... or not been?

    - How rigid were you?

    - Perhaps your mess wasn't being too rigid but rather too fluid? (Stand for something, or fall for everything.)

- Build or review your decision-making matrix.

    - What's on it? Is it simply your gut? (If so, that's not good enough.)

    - Do you have a process for how you make marketing investments, what you prioritize, what you say no to?

    - Recognize that experience and intuition are valuable, as long as they aren't the only two choices on your matrix.

- Consider establishing a management team, campaign board of advisors, or similar committee that can help formalize some decision-making criteria.

- Check your ego and be willing to change your position on a topic if necessary.

    - Explain why your position has evolved, while soliciting questions or comments from your team and other stakeholders.

    - Set the standard that your reputation isn't based on being right; rather, on being reasonable and open to growth.

    - Learn the delicate balance of confidence and vulnerability (which is how I often define leadership).

CHALLENGE 15

FRIEND YOUR COMPETITION

Do you view the competition as "kill or be killed," or can you allow for a "win-win"?

Not so long ago, it was a marketing and sales competency to pit yourself against your competition by finding their weaknesses and exploiting them. It was part of your job to ensure a potential customer knew all about your competitor's flaws and found them toxic by meeting's end. In many businesses, that was the value proposition: that your competitors sucked. How pitiful. That was a crutch, not a selling point.

Largely gone are the trash-talking days of dressing down your competition. Clients are much savvier now, to everyone's benefit. The democratization of information has empowered buyers, and most have researched your product or service online and in great detail. A recent study found that 97 percent of consumers consult product reviews (85 percent of them seeking negative reviews) before making a purchase, and over one-third of brick-and-mortar shoppers won't purchase a product before consulting reviews first.[13]

The concept of becoming your client's "trusted advisor" has had a great run in many sales forces, but I've not seen it as much in marketing. Many marketing teams are insulated from working directly with clients, and we get most of our market information from sales colleagues. Breaking free from this marketing mess requires that we think more abundantly. This is so important that I wrote about it in *Management Mess to Leadership Success* (Challenge 2: "Think Abundantly"). As a marketer, I've taken risks and often reaped the rewards when thinking more abundantly. And one success I'm most proud of is the rejection of the old paradigm of seeing your competition as "your enemy" and extending a hand of friendship instead. Friending your competition might sound Pollyanna-ish to some of you, but I think it's a fundamental business-and-leadership principle rarely practiced in marketing… or in most business divisions for that matter.

One of my competitors (and more importantly, friends) is Mary McChesney. But before we meet her, a little context. Utah is well known for incubating several industries. Drive the I-15 corridor, the 50 miles from

---

13   (2019) "Report: The Growing Power of Reviews." *Power Reviews*, 15 Feb., Available from: https://www.powerreviews.com/insights/growing-power-of-reviews/.

Salt Lake City to Provo, and you won't believe how many massive direct sales organizations (formally known as multilevel marketing companies, or MLMs) are headquartered here, often with attached manufacturing plants. NuSkin, Younique, dōTERRA, USANA, Young Living, and countless others are on the rise. I'm not involved in the direct-sales industry, but many I know who are have had success (and I suspect lost or fatigued a few friends and family in the process). Want to make your mother-in-law scarce? Join an essential-oil or nutrition company and talk about it every day for three months.

Utah is also a robust launchpad for leadership-development and performance-improvement companies. We seem to be the incubator for many of the world's best minds in personal and professional development. FranklinCovey was founded here, along with InsideOut Development, The Arbinger Institute, Partners in Leadership, Acumen Learning, and dozens of small up-and-coming boutique firms. One I'm very fond of, and a key competitor to FranklinCovey, is VitalSmarts, the company behind the wildly popular book *Crucial Conversations*. I highly recommend this book, and although I've not been through their training offerings, we have mutual clients who rave about VitalSmarts' solutions. Having attended one of their conferences, I was impressed at the quality experience they produced and how much they invest in their clients' success.

Enter Mary.

Mary McChesney serves as the vice president of marketing for VitalSmarts, which is an equivalent role to my own at FranklinCovey. Although privately held and significantly smaller, they compete with us for budget share with current and potential clients. Plainly put, they are a chief competitor. And I couldn't recommend them more highly if their solution exactly matches your problem.

About five years ago, I was meeting with some of our senior sales associates in Northern California and listening to their business development, positioning, messaging, and marketing needs. Over lunch, the conversation turned to our own brand and how it was received in the high-tech Silicon Valley area. I was told our content was highly valued and viewed as relevant by these fast, progressive tech companies, but that our brand was seen as "old" because their perception was that we still relied mainly on printed guidebooks for our work sessions. This was actually a false perception, as we were leading the industry in online, blended, and self-paced learning; but for some reason, that had escaped the awareness of the high-tech sector. Personally, I blame marketing. What buffoon was running that division at the time?

In one of these meetings, I was told by a salesperson, "VitalSmarts is kicking our butt in high tech because of how accessible their digital solutions are to a younger audience, and we need to do something about it."

We had, in fact, been doing something about it for the better part of a decade by investing millions of dollars into cutting-edge technologies, but we clearly hadn't told our story well or demonstrated the breadth of our digital capabilities to this sector of the market. So we set out to design a charm offensive whereby we could show these high-tech companies (most were not current clients) how flexible we were while demonstrating our unrivaled (both then and now) array of intellectual property. In addition, I contemplated what a shamed CMO should do when the field hands you your butt on a platter. Resisting the temptation to think of our competitor as the enemy, I invested time to learn more deeply about their competencies and approach to the marketplace. Obviously, I was aware of them, but when you're a dominant player in the industry, like FranklinCovey is, your hubris can catch you off guard. So after better understanding their value proposition, I sent their top marketing leader an email.

I didn't know Mary. I'd never met her; we had few or no LinkedIn mutual connections, so my email was a shot in the dark. Admittedly, it was a bold move: I invited her to lunch. *Oh, the horror! This isn't done!* Maybe chief learning officers can get away with this, or chief human-resources officers, but not CMOs. Product development, marketing, and sales strategies are sacrosanct. Loose lips sink ships.

Welcome to my career.

I'm pleased to admit those limiting thoughts never entered my mind—I simply wanted to meet the person responsible for kicking my butt and learn from her. To Mary's credit, she responded to my outreach. (Later she told me she consulted with her CEO for his perspective on meeting with me.) We met for lunch, both a bit guarded at first, declared our mutual intent, set some boundaries, and just dove in. This first meeting turned into five-plus years of periodic lunches where we responsibly shared our best practices and failures.

We both held our loyalties to our employers, surreptitiously subscribed to each other's newsletters, attended each other's webcasts, etc. We quickly realized we could learn a vast amount from each other without ever compromising our fiduciary responsibilities, mine especially as an officer in a public company. Mary would question me about improving the call to action in their emails and I would call her about their selection criteria for a marketing automation system. When someone from our firm would apply to theirs, and the reverse, we would call each other and confidentially vet the applicants (without ever discussing it with anyone else). Soon we invited colleagues to the lunches and helped each other in areas our teams were struggling with.

I truly came to admire and like Mary. Neither of us ever crossed a line or tried to trick the other into disclosing something sensitive or proprietary. On occasion we'd simply say we couldn't discuss an issue and move off it. We never socialized personally, but a highlight of this synergy was receiving an invitation to bring my wife and boys to her home for a holiday cookie-decorating party with her own children. I was honored—touched, really.

FranklinCovey is quantifiably better off because of this relationship with Mary. Some of the insights our team and I took from her created improvements and efficiencies where we were then less effective. I owe the prevention of a possible massive selection error in our marketing-automation vendor to Mary's own hard-earned vetting process and am grateful for her guidance on that issue.

As to the butt-kicking FranklinCovey and I were getting in Silicon Valley, our strategy to better compete was a direct outcome of my time spent with Mary. We created a two-hour, C-level-only invitation event based on my time learning from her. We directed our aim at fifty-plus tech companies where we showcased our world-class competencies in the most industry-relevant, progressive, and truthful manner possible. It was a home run, with more than two hundred executives showing up. Our pipeline of prospects from that experience built a marketing-event model we took to forty cities across the nation. To date, we've had over seven thousand prospects attend our "Culture, Your Ultimate Competitive Advantage" event. These engagements helped transform our brand in the eyes of many future clients, and helped me turn a marketing mess into a brand success.

When I decided to write this book, I gathered an initial list of forty challenges marketers faced and called Mary (among others) to vet them. Mary suggested several topics that proved to be very valuable. I've included them in the final thirty challenges found in this book and invited her to write her side of the story as well. She agreed, and it's below.

> Five or so years ago, I'd taken a chance and accepted Scott's lunch invitation because I was intrigued he had reached out cold. Surely there had to be something to learn from my counterpart at one of our top competitors. And there was!

> He drove over an hour to meet me for lunch that first time, graciously accepted my suggestion of where to meet (although as I've become more acquainted with him over the years, I realize he would have never chosen that restaurant), asked smart questions, seemed genuinely interested in helping me find value in the meeting, and paid the check. Not bad for my first foray into friending the competition, right?

> One interesting dynamic of our lunch conversations was the subsequent dialogue that ensued in the halls of VitalSmarts once I told people I was having lunch with the CMO at FranklinCovey. Some people were confused, "Wait, you're friendly with him?" Some were excited and saw it as an opportunity, "Oh, next time you talk to Scott, ask him about XYZ and let me know what he says!"

The funniest reaction was from some of the newer employees at VitalSmarts who had recently come from the tech industry. They looked shocked. "Mary, people in tech would *never* do that! That's unheard of." I reassured them all was well and no trade secrets were being divulged in some dark corner of a bar in West Valley, Utah.

One of the main takeaways from my "lunches with Scott," as they are called at VitalSmarts, was that you can friend your competition in a way that's transparent, honest, helpful, and downright fun. It turns out there's never a shortage of interesting topics to discuss when you're sitting across the table from someone who spends his or her workday in the same role and industry as you. And this may sound nerdy, but there's a palpable energy buzz when talking shop about marketing with someone like-minded.

Additionally, the perspective I gained from this friendship was immensely valuable—even if it was as simple as seeing my work from someone else's vantage point. If I got pushback on an idea, I'd often bring it up with Scott to see if his organization had run into something similar. If I was stuck on how to handle a situation, he was generous with his knowledge and experience. Often he'd validate something we were doing and provide me with an extra boost of confidence to move forward.

VitalSmarts and FranklinCovey compete for both wallet share and market share on a daily basis. We aren't strangers to competition. And yet, I like to believe we've nurtured a collaborative friendship that has benefited both organizations over the past few years. I think Scott would call that a win-win.

FROM MESS TO SUCCESS:

FRIEND YOUR COMPETITION

- Scan your industry competitors and make a list of those colleagues in similar or even more senior roles.

  - Depending on your own professional stature, consider connecting with them via LinkedIn and begin reading and consuming any of their posts and blog articles.

  - Determine who might be worth developing a relationship with.

- Consult with your leader if an outreach might be unconventional in your industry or with your employer.

  - Declare your intent that you're simply looking to connect and learn with others in the industry. Every organization has a different culture and view of their competition, so navigate those political waters wisely and transparently.

  - If approved, be bold and reach out to prospective competitors via email, a phone call, or a LinkedIn InMail.

- Cultivate mutually beneficial relationships with peers in both competitive and noncompetitive industries.

  - You may function as a director of marketing in the pharmaceutical industry but could benefit greatly from friending someone in a similar role in hospitality or food services.

  - Identify the areas of your own role you're looking to build expertise in and find those colleagues who might benefit you the most, recognizing, as in all relationship building, you need to add value to them as well.

CHALLENGE 16

NEVER FORGET YOU HAVE TWO BUYERS

Have you underestimated the influence of your internal buyers because you're only focused on your external buyers?

I've seen ignorance of this principle trip up countless marketing leaders. They think their key and only outcome is to please the external customer. And let's be honest, it's an understandably legitimate mindset, because they're paying the bills. But in the marketing field, where everyone has an opinion, ignoring your internal constituency is a guaranteed mess that paves the way to your career's death—a mess easily avoided, however, if you keep one ear to the ground and listen to your multiple stakeholders.

This principle, never forgetting you have two buyers, stands whether your marketing efforts support a sales staff of three hundred or you're a lone wolf working in a small business and reporting to the owner. You always have two buyers: internal and external. Seems like a *duh* at first blush, but both have very different profiles, needs, attention spans, and ways in which they voice their support or dissent. I want to dedicate this challenge to the first buyer who's often neglected or completely forgotten about by marketing: your internal buyers.

Internal buyers are anyone and everyone who has an opinion on what you do. It's such a long list, you'd quit on the spot if you wrote it all out. Again, welcome to marketing. It's reasonable (and frustrating) that nobody really has an opinion on accounting's quarter-close process, or product development's Q/A testing sequence. Nor do most people really care if SAP or Oracle becomes your ERP provider. But a point worth repeating is that *everyone* has an opinion about marketing. Better to acknowledge this and build your charm offensive now than to be naïve and caught off guard.

I invite you to take a few moments and list those people (perhaps even by name) in your organization who are in fact "buyers" of your marketing efforts. It doesn't mean they actually spend money, but they have other valuable currency (influence). Consider some of these profiles inside your organization:

- Someone who has the positional power to unilaterally veto your idea or campaign.

- The person who lacks formal authority but has cultural power or influence to bring your campaign to a halt.

- A salesperson or leader whose income is directly tied to the success of your efforts (not to mention hitting their monthly/quarterly/annual sales targets).

- The junior finance associate who will review or approve the budget supporting your strategy, or worse, dissect it in private with their leader and in lightning speed become the most powerful person in your world. When I say "powerful," I really mean "hated."

Take a moment and fill out your internal-buyer list. As I'm an advocate for writing between the lines, dog-earing pages, and otherwise scribbling notes so this book truly becomes yours (you e-book readers will just have to hit the "notes" button; and audio listeners, go ahead and grab paper and pen.) Use the following scale: (1 = low, 10 = high).

MY POTENTIAL INTERNAL BUYERS

(Not to be confused with the "Colleagues I Like and Dislike List")

Name	Role	Formal or informal influence (1–10)	State of my relationship with them (1–10)	Do I need to invite them to the process or charm them through the process? (1–10)

Did you do it, or just skip to this section? If you skipped ahead, I challenge you to go back and fill out the table (unless you've checked the book out of the library, in which case I give you permission to photocopy the table and do it later).

Finished now? Great. I get that this is an overly simplistic look at the politics of your marketing team, but it's invaluable for you to be aware of the forces operating both vocally and silently so you can decide if and how you plan to address them. A word of caution: You could easily become obsessed with managing all the shifting winds coming your way and never achieve liftoff, or more importantly, the financial results you signed your campaign up for. Don't forget about your *second* buyer as you work to strike the right balance between the two. As you become increasingly aware of two concepts shared in this book—first, "It's the Customer, Stupid"; and second, "How to Orbit the Giant Hairball"—you'll gain the perspective and insight to find that balance.

One of the most significant lessons I've learned in my marketing career is about the timing and environment for pitching your next approach/campaign/initiative/launch/save-the-day-most-creative-marketing idea. Never—I repeat *never*—gather your internal group of stakeholders together in the same conference room, meeting, phone call, Skype, or Zoom session and pitch it to them simultaneously as your "out of the gate" strategy. No marketing campaign will die a faster death than at the hands of the fickleness of critical groupthink. All it takes is one opinion leader to express a concern, and like piranhas around a carcass, your initiative will be feverously torn apart. The odds that you will recover are slim, and I've learned that when certain leaders "smell blood in the water," their baser instincts take over (and sadly, some find delight in the carnage).

Here's my hard-earned advice: divide and conquer.

When you've identified your list of vital, internal buyers for your next project—it might be as small as two and as large as ten—refer to your list and call or meet with them individually in a strategic sequence. Yes, that may mean ten meetings as opposed to one. That can be fatiguing, but the payoff is absolutely worth it, and I've never regretted the time and energy invested in it. I have done this countless times, and it directly correlates with the level of success I've achieved at winning, early on, the support of those exact people who would have opposed the idea or torn it apart had I given them a platform to peacock among a group of their peers. By having individual conversations, it allowed me to satisfy the WIIFM (What's in It for Me?) and allowed my colleagues to ask questions about viability, budget, success factors, etc., which I could then fine-tune for the next conversation. No one ever felt like I was playing them, because I wasn't. I was simply practicing a time-tested, diplomatic tactic that allowed me to fact-find privately (and candidly, refine my own thinking along the way) while validating that I recognized their need to be involved. Try this. It's a nearly foolproof strategy to win over your internal buyers. I term it "Focus Grouping to the One."

Ironically, the idea of separating one person from the "pack" to hold a high-stakes conversation is the same advice shared with me by a colleague who spent a summer working with gang members out of Los Angeles. Their bravado and need to grandstand in front of their peers diminished substantially when isolated and allowed to talk one-on-one. Yes, I just compared seasoned professionals to inner-city gang members. Call it "Wall Street" meets *West Side Story* with slightly less finger snapping.

The main insight from employing the divide-and-conquer strategy is that by the time you do bring them together as a group (and that's inevitable), no one is ambushed and everyone feels some level of inclusion and validation. When legitimate challenges now surface, they're made with different motives: to clarify, tighten, and perfect; not to obfuscate, expose, or undermine. Because you've paid the price to bring them into the tent early, they're already in your camp. The question is no longer "Should we build a fire?" but "Where, when, and how big?"

Your skill at this will come with time, some real-world lessons, and an increasing discernment about whom to pay attention to and whom to ignore. Since many marketers forget to serve the internal customer, use your list to help minimize the mess of hijacked momentum and instead build a flywheel of support that drives success.

FROM MESS TO SUCCESS:

NEVER FORGET YOU HAVE TWO BUYERS

- Determine how many internal "buyers" you have.

  - Do you need to care about them all? No marketing leader wants to become consumed with politicking all day and building support for their campaigns—but it's a very important part of their role. Ignore it at your own peril.

- Build coalitions of supportive constituencies.

  - Identify who are the "must haves" on your side. Is it the same group for every campaign, or different?

  - Use your coalition to not only progress your marketing vision, but to ensure the vision is the right one to pursue for the organization.

- Recognize how your internal and external buyers will often fatigue at very different paces.

  - Internal stakeholders will generally become bored much more quickly with messaging, initiatives, and campaigns than the external market of prospects.

  - Become adept at pinpointing when internal stakeholders are bored or restless.

  - Determine when and if you're changing strategies merely to keep their attention. Not always a bad idea, just acknowledge it to yourself and your team.

CHALLENGE 17

HIRE PEOPLE SMARTER THAN YOU

Are you confident and vulnerable enough to not always be the smartest person in the room?

Here comes the biggest mess of my career. It's not unique to marketing, but I hope the lesson learned stays with you throughout your entire professional journey as it took me the better part of thirty years to learn it. If you grasp the full horror of my mess, it will change the way you lead, hire, coach, collaborate, create, design, and communicate with others.

I don't want to exaggerate this point, but I had an epiphany during my last year as chief marketing officer. I didn't know it would be my last year at the time. The fact is, I could still be in the role if I had chosen to, but for a variety of reasons, I made the decision to step away and pursue other interests both inside and outside the company. That sounds like the boiler-plate explanation you'd hear from a CEO just forced out due to a plummeting stock price or some personal indiscretion. Neither was the case for me. I had built significant capacity among the marketing team, and the vice president reporting to me was very capable to not only lead, but take the team in a new direction—a direction that was better aligned with what the new company president needed as he was leading a radical change, for the better, in our go-to-market strategy.

The CEO asked me to stay in the role; perhaps he was just being gracious, but three requests usually equates more with confidence than harmony. Regardless, I stepped aside and never looked back. I did, however, reflect on my leadership style and came to see a major flaw (i.e., a mess)—one that, in all candor and with the benefit of hindsight, likely lessoned the impact of our marketing efforts and certainly my own influence as a leader.

Grab a tumbler and some scotch—you might need a few fingers to make it through this one. On second thought, I'll do it for you, as I may need a little liquid courage to lay my mess bare.

Twenty-four years ago, when I moved to Utah from Orlando, Florida, it was a rough transition, one of the most difficult and emotional of my life. As a single Catholic guy from a very diverse town in central Florida who moved to Provo, Utah, I would liken it to being an Orthodox Jew relocating to Vatican City. Great for a sabbatical, but likely not worth declaring residency and getting a library card. At the time, Provo was over 80 percent populated by Mormons (formally known as members of The

Church of Jesus Christ of Latter-day Saints). The novelty was great for the first two months, but beyond that, it became fatiguing—I'm guessing for them too.

How does this relate to my actions nearly twenty-five years later? Oh, it's inextricably linked, and I didn't even hire a therapist to uncover it. I've come to realize that one of my coping strategies for living and thriving in a very exclusive culture (like that of a country club where you're either "in" or you're "out" and no one is confused about their membership status) was to build a very thick skin, making sure I was always the smartest person in the room and wasn't a good candidate for a missionary discussion. This combination of "don't tread on me" and a propensity to intellectually fence my way out of any intimidating situation no doubt resulted in my mess of being unwilling to hire people smarter than I was.

I don't begin to blame anyone for my messes, but as I unpack them and become both more vulnerable and more willing to openly share, it's been helpful to pinpoint where my belief system changed or mindset leaned one way or another.

As the chief marketing officer for FranklinCovey, I came to believe I was the most capable member of the marketing team. Not necessarily an expert in every topic, but because the "buck stopped with me," I felt the need to own everything. I was effective enough at collaborating and allowing others to brainstorm, but ultimately, I was the company's secret weapon—the creative genius sitting over in marketing outdoing himself every quarter, twenty-five quarters in a row and counting.

How absurdly arrogant.

Was I successful at a few things? Through the key leadership of many, including myself, we drove significant growth in market share and EBITDA, and our stock price more than quadrupled—all while the culture of the marketing team seemed to be fraying. When the leader of any team believes they are the smartest person in the room, there's a systemic issue in play that at some point will implode. But some implosions unfold slowly without obvious spectacle or collateral damage. Slowly enough, in fact, that they aren't even noticeable at the time. Or maybe I'm still fooling myself.

The arrogance that drove this thinking resulted in my sometimes hiring associates whom I believed were less talented than I was. (In hindsight, they were probably vastly more talented than I gave them credit for.) In my view, they were talented enough to bring value, but not so talented as to challenge my own position or contribution as the creative genius running marketing. I fear I didn't always seek to hire those who had world-class expertise in their respective areas, as they could challenge my sometimes tenuous credibility. Conversely, I hired people whose personalities I liked—those I thought I could collaborate with and possessed strong character, but ultimately wouldn't overreach their respective places on the team and expose my facade. To again reference Liz Wiseman, author of *Multipliers*, I was the classic example of being the genius, not the genius maker of others. I inherently feared other talented marketers and assumed they would eclipse me—or worse, expose me. Let me clarify: As I reflect, I suspect I unconsciously hired people whom I didn't feel threatened by and passed on those I did. In my vast insecurity, I didn't want anyone to eclipse my value to the firm and, as a result, I likely diminished and suppressed otherwise very talented people's intellect and contributions.

Because of my insecurity around the seismic technological impact disrupting marketing, I became a bit paralyzed over where to focus first. As a result, I likely didn't move as fast as was necessary, as I feared making major missteps that might threaten my stature in the company. Consequently, I didn't identify and recruit outside expertise swiftly enough either. Up until then, much of my tenure and influence had been based on avoiding fiascos and black holes, and generally staying clear of technological boondoggles that could sink me or the company. Thus, my hesitancy to install progressive technology platforms and hire highly technical people was brought on by… me. Instead, I should have deliberately sought out experts in social media, predictive analytics, SEO, marketing automation, and other emerging technologies of which I had little to no knowledge, other than that we needed them.

Did we miss the boat altogether? Of course not. We implemented Marketo (a robust marketing-automation platform), built our social channels, and thinned our sites, making them much more navigable. But candidly, it was all a minimum effort to keep the naysayers off my back. This was clearly not my strong suit, and my insecurities around it slowed our traction.

I admit it. I've learned from my self-imposed mess. The team has thrived and long since moved on, and the ground they've covered is remarkable. I am proud of them. But I'm also proud of myself for recognizing that my limiting paradigms were grounded in my own insecurity. And I'm proud of myself for having the courage to let the team thrive and grow beyond my genius (i.e., arrogance). It wasn't easy to leave a significant and secure role.

I share this mess to challenge your own willingness to hire people smarter than you. As the leader in marketing, your key contribution (depending on the size and scope of your team) is to ensure you're recruiting and retaining the best possible talent—associates who are noticeably more talented than you and have expertise in their own areas that you could never compete with or have any need to.

I attended a marketing conference several years back, and one of the CMOs on the panel said something profound about the role. She challenged us to view ourselves as the CRO: not the chief revenue officer, but rather the chief *recruitment* officer. As the CRO, your charge is to build a brand where the absolute best talent begs to come and stay. But it's hard to do that when you're the genius and stuck in your own limiting mess.

So I send you off with a challenge—perhaps even the biggest challenge of your own marketing career. Are you courageous enough to hire the best, most talented associates who eclipse your own talent so much that everyone in the organization wonders why you even work there? That's the ultimate test and your ultimate contribution.

Finally, let me bring this confessional train safely into the station. I don't know how much of my move to Utah really contributed to my hubris and inability to deliberately hire people smarter than I. My guess is some, but not entirely. So I formally release all of my LDS friends from my psychosis—I own it. Thank you for the tremendous value (and green Jell-O) you've added to my life. Like many of you reading this, I suffer from the well-known professional ailment known as imposter syndrome. No doubt, you've got your own train full of crazy; and if my sold-out, standing-room-only cabin gives you some permission to acknowledge yours and pull the brake, then mission accomplished.

FROM MESS TO SUCCESS:

HIRE PEOPLE SMARTER THAN YOU

- Assess your need to be the smartest person in the room and determine how it might be diminishing others. Ask a trusted colleague to monitor when they see you in meetings flipping back into this pattern so you're mindful of what, and who, triggers you.

  - Determine if any of your go-to strengths are holding others back.

  - Are you suppressing the marketing ideas, creativity, career aspirations, or solutions that could help your brand, growth, and customers?

- If you find your need to be the "smartest" is a pattern, take time to be introspective about it. Ask:

  - What might be driving me to feel insecure about my talents and contributions?

  - Am I bringing fears from my personal life or perhaps a previous career into my current marketing role?

  - Do I think I already "know it all" when it comes to marketing and so have nothing left to learn?

  - What would happen if I substituted being the "smartest" in the room with being my "best self" in the room? What would I say and do differently?

CHALLENGE 18

LEAVE THE STUNTS TO HOLLYWOOD

Is your confidence in your product or service so tepid you're considering stunts to heat things up?

In 2007, a video-marketing company had what they thought was a genius idea. In an effort to promote their client's television program (*Aqua Teen Hunger Force*), they placed a series of thirty-eight light boards around Boston with a figure waving a middle finger. Massive chaos erupted as the city came to a halt. Bridges were closed, boat traffic on the Charles River was suspended, and a citywide bomb scare ensued. Eventually, it was discovered that the light boards were part of a guerrilla marketing campaign by a New York-based advertising/marketing firm and, in fact, they'd placed similar boards throughout seventeen other U.S. cities. Arrests were made and officials still refer to the incident as a "bomb hoax" to this day.

Unfortunately, this mess wasn't enough to stop other well-intentioned marketers from pulling their own similarly ridiculous stunts. To that end, here are some fundamental truths in marketing to be strongly considered:

- If you're a software company, and in a moment of insanity your CEO is tempted to showcase the new app or program live, in front of any audience, distract them with some emergency (perhaps call and have their Range Rover towed from the parking lot). Such live demonstrations rarely work when relying on a Wi-Fi connection. Bandwidth in a conference hall with six thousand people all pulling on it simultaneously will never be like it was during your office demo the day before (or even during your sound check thirty minutes before the doors opened). DO NOT ATTEMPT THIS unless you are sadistic and would love to watch your CEO implode. Instead, build other acceptable workarounds. Screen shots can look remarkably real. Or better, just acknowledge the risk of unstable networks and talk straight, explaining that you're going to use a deck to demo your awesome tool. People will love your transparency.

- If you're the manufacturer of ubercool, battery-operated cars and are in the process of introducing your new truck and its "unbreakable windows," DO NOT throw a rock at it in front of a live audience. Since everyone will be live-streaming your stunt, the resulting crash will be the sound of your brand shattering around the world. Okay, maybe only for a moment if your brand is otherwise reputable, but some will always associate you and your products with the fiasco, regardless of whether or not your car company becomes the most valuable in the world—especially when the video goes viral and you fuel rumors that it was all planned. People aren't idiots.

- If you ask Hollywood director Michael Bay (*Transformers*) to come share the stage with you as your latest TV technology is unveiled at the renowned Consumer Electronics Show in Las Vegas, don't encourage him to just "wing it" when his monitor goes out. Because not only will a surprised celebrity not stay on message, they won't even stay on the stage. (He turned and walked off.) Oh, you've got to Google this one (keywords: Michael Bay, Samsung, CES).

Stunts are classic groupthink. Your product or service can't stand on its own, so a well-intended yet inexperienced team member cooks up a plan to "shock and awe" your way to free publicity. Nearly all of stunts like this fail. They either aren't noticed, or they get noticed for the wrong reasons. Rarely, if ever, do stunts win you that long-term result you wanted and signed up for.

Here's a mess of my own; although not a stunt per se, it certainly shares something in common with the Boston light-board example.

For nearly a decade, I've partnered with an outside printing company who runs fulfillment for many of our marketing collateral, brochures, invitations, event workbooks, conference signage, etc. It's an ideal collaboration led by Kelly Thompson from Alexander's Printing in Utah. Kelly isn't your standard print salesperson. The year I hired him as a vendor, he won Utah's Salesperson of the Year. Also an entrepreneur, he invented a cutting tool for crafters named Cutterpillar. Check it out at cutterpillar.com. Kelly is a superb partner, anticipating my needs and even bringing me samples of new and innovative campaigns he's seen applied in other industries. He is such a trusted vendor that he has a security badge and can pretty much roam our entire campus, which drives our purchasing department nuts. His value to our company is indisputable. (If you want a great creative print or campaign partner, email Kelly at kellyt@ alexanders.com and tell him Scott sent you!)

One day, Kelly walked into our offices, beaming, and whipped out a small package the size of a five-by-seven printed photo. When he opened it, I realized it was a marketing tool for a Bentley—the British automobile on par with Rolls Royce (some might say even better). It resembled one of those greeting cards that play a short song when opened. In this case, a portion of the card had a built-in video screen the size of a credit card, and you could watch three separate one-minute videos about Bentley.

It was visually captivating. Not so much because of the video content or quality (which was exceptional—if someone from Bentley is reading this, please contact my publicist about working out a deal), but I was intrigued by the fact that the technology to watch a series of high-resolution videos in a portable and, ultimately, disposable foldout card existed. Kelly had additional samples, one for a European currency conversion firm and another for a pharma company. Basically, he had me at hello. Plus the video card had what I call in marketing "the guilt factor," meaning nobody could ever throw it out, and anyone receiving it would be compelled to show it to countless colleagues as they kept it on their desks far after the campaign's timeline.

Like many marketing ideas, when I am exposed to them in some form or fashion, it may be some time before I choose to use them. I might see lettering or a color scheme on a menu or billboard and choose to use it a quarter or a year later. This happened with the video cards. They percolated in my mind for a few months and then, as we were preparing for a forty-city tour featuring Stephen M. R. Covey, author of *The Speed of Trust*, we decided to create a video-card campaign. Our plan was to include several videos about Stephen's content and then deliver them to carefully chosen CEOs who, we hoped, might watch the video and decide to come to the local event. Because the cards cost about thirty dollars

MARKETING MESS TO BRAND SUCCESS

each, we were careful in developing our list of C-suite invitees. We ran the idea past Stephen, and although we all agreed it was a bit decadent (okay, completely over the top), we thought it a solid investment if it got the attention of otherwise impossible-to-reach CEOs.

The cards worked exceptionally well, the tour was a massive hit, and C-level clients registered in droves. Nearly every one of them commented positively on the card.

Except one.

They were a well-known firearms manufacturer, a target client for FranklinCovey, and I believe their headquarters was in the northeast. Because some of the identified CEOs lived outside the driving distance of our field sales staff, we mailed about 20 percent of the video cards to them. One day, midway into the campaign, our regional sales leader received a call from the local police. Apparently, the firearms manufacturer scans all of their incoming mail for security reasons, and the video card was flagged as a potential explosive. Within minutes, the ATF, FBI, state police, and local law enforcement were onsite with a bomb disposal unit for what was thought to be a bomb scare. Our video card, featuring Stephen M. R. Covey extolling the benefits of organizational trust, ended up in the hands of highly suspicious ATF and FBI agents. It made the local news (not ours fortunately), and as soon as the details were made to me, I found myself doing preventive damage control with the CEO, CFO, and the member of our board who owned risk management. The image in my mind of an agent wearing a bomb suit carefully opening a card to be greeted with a friendly video message illustrating "The 13 Behaviors of High-Trust Leaders" from Stephen M. R. Covey still haunts me.

It all ended without issue (I wasn't arrested or flagged in a Homeland Security watch list), and even our local contact at the targeted company eventually agreed the marketing idea was innovative.

Not a stunt in the truest sense, it certainly could have brought our firm some bad PR if less calm and deliberate professionals had handled it differently. The CEO from the firearms manufacturer never came to our event on organizational trust, but I learned two valuable lessons:

First, think carefully through any unintended consequences of your campaigns. Second, only hand-deliver your video cards.

You can avoid your own marketing mess by skipping stunts altogether. Instead, invest time in perfecting your offering and how you responsibly (and innovatively) communicate it to your smallest viable market (see Challenge 11). And while we're on the topic, don't ever use the word "viral." Nothing you do is ever going to go viral. I've never met a CMO who developed a campaign that went viral because they said it would. There's an inverse correlation between your intent to "go viral" and what actually does—the harder you try, the less it will. Unless, of course, you include a cat or a baby lip-syncing. Then you're golden.

Some of you may skip this advice because you're suffering from a rapidly shortening cash runway, so you've declared, "Why not just go for it?" Good luck to you. And you'll need what little cash remains after your stunt fails; or worse, harms someone and you end up with an invoice from the county sheriff and a subpoena from the local prosecutor. Law enforcement generally lacks the same humor gene that convinced you *your* stunt, despite all evidence to the contrary, was going to go great.

I get that it's increasingly difficult to separate your voice from the pack and nearly impossible to get your prospect's attention. That's why this particular marketing mess is so tempting. But your job is to resist "itching the scratch" that results from a need to be outrageously creative, provocative, or attention-grabbing. And remember, what I might think is a stunt might well become the new norm and be a yawner for the next generation. So please proceed with great caution and don't think up "light boards" alone in your office. Or if you do, at least run it up a sage's proverbial flagpole for some feedback.

Remember, everything and everyone is only six simple letters away: G-o-o-g-l-e.

FROM MESS TO SUCCESS:

LEAVE THE STUNTS
TO HOLLYWOOD

- Don't do them.

- Resist the continued urge to do them.

- You're acquiescing to pressure from the team and are thinking about doing them. Don't.

- Recommit to *never* doing them.

- If the owner of your company directs you to lead a stunt or you'll be fired, follow these directions:

  - Retain legal counsel.

  - Change your name and strip any references to your current employment from your social accounts.

  - Grow a beard and wear a hat.

  - Refuse and call their bluff.

  - Find a new career. You're working for the wrong company.

CHALLENGE 19

CHOOSE THE RIGHT MEASURES

Are you measuring what matters?

Marketing may well be the last organizational division to leverage metrics in turning what has historically been an art into much more of a science. Oracle and SAP brought enormous efficiencies to finance and operations; Salesforce.com transformed sales pipelines and forecasting; and Adobe and others are reinventing marketing. For a century plus, much of marketing was impressions, influence, and building awareness—very difficult-to-measure metrics, and I think it's fair to say historically many marketers probably liked that because it was hard to pin them down and make them prove ROI. The capabilities of predictive analytics have changed the level of accountability, the profile of people hired to join marketing teams, and the way the C-suite is able to analyze the impact marketing has directly (or indirectly) on revenue, customer engagement, and brand equity.

Yes, predictive analytics has changed the marketing landscape, but don't let that scare you too much. I've met my share of analytic experts who are quite pleased to measure all of *your* campaigns and tell you how wrong you are, yet couldn't build a marketing strategy of their own that would impress my elementary school sons. I liken to it when finance decides to school the sales division on how best to make their quarter. Enough said. I don't want to piss off finance too terribly much.

Remember the adage "Those who can, do. Those who can't, teach. And those who really can't, consult." Oh my, the emails about to come my way... We need all those smart data wonks to provide us predictive measures with which to constantly calibrate our effectiveness. But be careful not to surrender the creativity, vision, and strategy to someone appropriately and myopically focused on data alone. Remember, data is one of many components in the marketing landscape. It's a vital point on the map—it's not *the* map. Increasingly, the collection and interpretation of quality data is not only instructive, but key to driving allocation of resources, timing of campaigns, segmentation of markets, the understanding of demographic preferences, and countless other areas necessary to increase the assurance that your message and strategy resonate with current and potential customers. Remember that marketing is a combination of head and heart. Instinct and analytics. Experience and vision. Data is part of the puzzle, not *the* puzzle.

Early in this book, I harped (perhaps too much) on the need for marketing to align with, support, and drive sales—even if it requires a formal alignment that subordinates marketing to sales. If I were to become the CEO of a company (maybe less likely now, after all the mess admissions), I would strongly consider connecting marketing to sales. Depending on the maturity and relationship of the sales and marketing leaders, it's often the best bet to ensure synergy, lessen or eliminate conflict, and sustain alignment and momentum between the two.

My position on this comes from a lifelong career balanced between both sales and marketing, and several decades watching duplicity, fear, and self-preservation drive too many decisions on both sides. From this perspective, I'll offer some steps for marketing leaders to consider as they build their metrics.

Define common terms and their meanings. One of the biggest messes I see in marketing divisions is the crazy marketing talk. I've often heard the phrase "If HR wants a 'seat at the table,' they need to stop the HR talk and speak the language of business instead." Perhaps a bit harsh, but still food for thought. The same should be said for marketing: stop the marketing talk and speak sales. Marketing professionals need to exercise more discipline in the words we use. A former sales leader of mine, Bill Bennett, once gave me some feedback on my leadership style that I've never forgotten: "Scott, call things by their proper names." It wasn't a reference to my vocabulary or communication style but more my propensity to exaggerate or embellish.

Hold your righteous judgment. We all do it, including you.

Yes, I'm a fairly colorful and demonstrative person. I'm proud of that and other "talents" that have served me well in life. But Bill was right—I needed to become more disciplined with my words and descriptions.

I've paid forward Bill's advice by sharing it with my team. Over the years, we've had many discussions on what it means to call things by their right names, like what constitutes a "lead." I can be quoted for often declaring, "A name is not a lead." Because someone walked up to the trade-show booth and you asked for their business card after a two-minute conversation, that does not correlate to a lead. Because someone registers for a webcast, or you met them at a chamber event, it does not qualify them as a lead. Names are names and leads are leads. And both will be defined differently in every organization. All names don't have the same value or accuracy in data records, and all leads won't have the same level of qualification or scoring. The good news is you get to decide. But be sure everyone in the marketing division—and those outside—are on the same page regarding how key terms are defined. Clarity is the key to both minimizing conflict and managing expectations, especially between sales and marketing, which should be two of the most interdependent divisions in any organization. It's quite common for marketing to think, "We've hit it out of the park," while sales is thinking, "Looks like another bunt."

Now, a chance for me to lean hard on sales. (Marketing leaders should take away both some validation and an opportunity for introspection from this next insight.) Another sales leader of mine termed it "Happy Ears": novice, inexperienced sales professionals learn quickly (hopefully) what's a real opportunity and what's not. Happy Ears is a concept many sales and marketing leaders see team members struggle with when they think everything is a hot lead, a certain sale, or a million-dollar, career-changing deal. Some advice: Never utter the words "hot lead" again. It's sort of like calling yourself an expert—if you *do*, you're clearly *not*. The fact that your anesthesiologist is an expert is a given. Being assured by *her* that she is an expert—on the way to the surgical room—will only raise more questions than answers.

Being aware of your Happy Ears tendencies doesn't mean you become a pessimist or lessen your dogged determinism to turn a sow's ear into a silk purse (proverbs from the 1500s may be making a comeback, so stay with me). Instead of Happy Ears, build a brand as a realist whereby your insights and instincts become golden. Learn the difference between when a name is just a name, and when a name is likely a lead—but never a hot one.

Key Takeaway: Invest the proactive time and effort to ensure marketing's terms, definitions, and understanding of the dashboard versus the scoreboard measures are the same as the divisions you're supporting. A little extra clarity on the front end can help avoid massive confusion and disappointment on the back end.

Avoid the fool's errand. When a name is just a name and marketing puts it in the CRM (Customer Relationship Management) system, assigns it to a salesperson to follow up on, and they do, you're done for. You've never experienced wrath like a commissioned salesperson who wasted an inordinate amount of time on your so-called "lead" only to find out it was a total dud. The absolute quickest way to kill your credibility with sales—especially with a seasoned, high-producing salesperson—is to send them on a fool's errand. Their Happy Ears were clipped long ago and their patience for this is zero!

In case it isn't obvious to you by now, *do not ever load business cards collected from a trade show, or badges scanned from a conference, or a registration list from a webcast into your CRM and present them as leads to be followed up on by the sales team.* If you're tempted or asked by someone else to do this, be sure the next site you visit after you do is Indeed.com.

Key Takeaway: Similar to the conundrum of Happy Ears, marketers don't want to fall into a similar sensory trap: the "Happy Nose." This is when you demonstrate your naivete and shallow experience around understanding when an opportunity is real versus when someone is simply being gracious or inquisitive. Be deliberate about what you "sniff out" as a lead and ask sales (or anyone for that matter) to spend their time pursuing. The worst combination any organization can suffer from is Happy Ears in sales and a Happy Nose in marketing, sending everyone running around and chasing their own tail.

Get agreement on the most vital metrics. Meet with your sales leadership, owner, or whoever is ultimately responsible for revenue and make sure you agree on the most important metrics. By definition, they are the ones that, when met, will be agreed upon as a win for all. Here's a disclaimer: I want to be sure that, throughout this book, I've not accidentally demonized marketing and lifted sales at their expense. Nothing could be further from my mindset. Sales is ultimately responsible for revenue, and in many cultures, they often have huge gaps in their own competencies: articulating their value proposition poorly, building and managing relationships improperly, crafting weak proposals, inaccurately entering data and opportunities into the database, forecasting inaccurately, and sometimes being unable to see (let alone close) a sale that falls right into their lap. I'll go much deeper into this topic in my *Sales Mess to Revenue Success* book, slated to be the fifth title in the *Mess to Success* series. And yes, I'll flog it (and myself) plenty! Until then, I want to reinforce that just because sales misses their number doesn't mean they will take full responsibility for it. Some sales leaders are tempted to sell out as many people as possible to prop up their own careers. But the clearer and more transparent you are about agreed-upon metrics, the more this should insulate you and your team from pitiful, incompetent, or pressured sales leaders trying to save their career at your expense.

Key Takeaway: Subtly but importantly different from agreeing on mutual definitions is the necessity of agreeing on your key metrics. Beyond agreement on the inputs, are we all in agreement on the outputs? Have we defined those critical success factors such that all stakeholders are clear when we've crossed the finish line? Nothing is more humiliating or career ending than marketing planting the flag and taking the photo fifty yards beneath the actual summit.

Be honest and realistic. When co-creating and confirming the metrics, be sure you feel comfortable that you have the assets and capabilities to achieve them. Be responsibly confident when pushing back against targets or campaign outcomes that you feel are unreasonable. Calm resistance, based on facts and logic, is often met with appreciation from mature and wise leaders. No principled leader wants to be surrounded by sycophants or people who say yes to everything while knowing all along the results will never come. And because such individuals lack the courage or diplomacy to resist, they don't deliver in the end and everyone is screwed. (This is not far-fetched, and it happens in every organization around the world every single day.) This type of culture is sadly very common in high-pressure sales environments. When you genuinely feel or know a goal is unattainable, say so. Your pushback needs to be defendable, and not a lame attempt to avoid hard work or stretching your skills. If you've earned credibility in other projects by overdelivering, you'll be seen as preventing a domino effect of disappointments later on. Great leaders don't want to be lied to, and too few understand when they themselves have built a culture that encourages it. This is often what precedes a cheating culture, and they always implode.

Key Takeaway: As a member of marketing, you will be continually faced with being seen as either part of the solution or part of the problem as it relates to supporting and signing up for heroic contributions. You will need to learn the delicate balance of achieving extraordinary results that seem unobtainable with prudently calling out (early on) the impossible when everyone in the room knows that's the case. Metrics and scoreboards, at the end of the day, are going to call you out, so don't cosign checks neither of you can cash.

Know the metrics predictive of success (revenue). Your metrics may well be spread across several mediums and channels. They could be clicks, opens, or conversions. They might be registrations, attendees, and follow-ups. With a sales force, they're likely tied to outbound prospecting, including activities focused on cold calls, emails sent, face-to-face meetings, and proposals submitted. The list is endless. One heads-up: Be sure you know which metrics are predictive of success. And when I say success, I mean revenue. At some point, you should be able to quantify how much "each dial is worth"—if you have twenty-three people registered for the lunch, that seventeen will show up, five will develop into solid prospects, and two will actually buy within ninety days. You know your industry best and your conversion rates will vary. But if you don't know them, start learning them and track them fiercely. Eventually, you'll have data and targets to build increasingly better campaigns upon. I am bewildered at how many sales organizations hire their sales staff, train them (a bit), and then throw them to the wolves, hoping they'll figure it out. The same often happens in marketing. Marketing must continually set and adjust relevant metrics and ensure all of your activities and team members' time and talents are focused on them.

Key Takeaway: As Einstein said, "If I had an hour to solve a problem and my life depended on the solution, I would spend the first fifty-five minutes determining the proper question to ask…for once I know the proper question, I could solve the problem in less than five minutes." Dedicate as much time to ensuring the metrics you're pursuing are valid and predictive of success as you do to interpreting the results.

Every organization has a different propensity for how diligently they want to set and align to key metrics. It's indisputable that the marketplace is increasingly basing nearly every significant bet and strategy on what the data shows. But there are flaws in that. Just ask Hillary Clinton. Concurrent with this momentum is the equally valid fact that we all know some things to "just be true"—what your instincts scream at you to follow. I've learned something valuable in my career, and this next line might be the most useful in the book:

Everyone's just making it up as they go.

That's a fairly all-encompassing statement, but there's more fact than fiction in it. If it *weren't* true, every organization would be using the same, indisputable playbook, every state would follow the same economic policy, every dentist would fill cavities the same way, and every NFL quarterback would throw the ball with the same technique. We're all guessing, second-guessing, doubling down, bailing, debating, trying something new, and pushing as far as we can without being called out (or worse found out). It's called imposter syndrome, and as I've previously disclosed, I have it—and so do you. And so does the vice president of sales, and the CIO, the CEO, and the seemingly untouchable members of your mysterious and all-powerful board of directors. That doesn't mean we all don't have valuable experience and haven't learned well-tested lessons along the way, or that we haven't achieved some significant successes that can be built upon. But don't be deluded into thinking you're the only person questioning your skills and strategy. Some are just faking it better than you are. Fear is part of the human condition. Lean into it.

When I was much younger, I was far too easily impressed with "successful" people, and I wasn't exactly a slouch myself. But as I've aged and been in countless boardrooms, private planes, executive luncheons, green rooms, and behind the scenes with hundreds of CEOs, celebrities, authors, and "experts" at all levels, they're all just you and me. Truly. It's likely they worked harder, tried one more time instead of bailing, or in most cases, didn't care what the detractors said about them and instead believed their own press.

So if this is all new and somewhat foreign to you, don't worry. Find your own balance, co-craft your metrics, and then go crush it! And on your way, throw that business-card scanner into the trash can.

FROM MESS TO SUCCESS:

CHOOSE THE RIGHT MEASURES

- Become adept at scoreboarding principles, including knowing the difference between lead and lag measures. By publishing a scoreboard for every stakeholder to see, you will reinforce the agreed-upon metrics by which everyone is defining success or failure.

- Determine what you are doing to expand your knowledge of the overall business and ensure you're business bilingual. Suggestions include:

    - Identify a coach or mentor in the finance, operations, sales, or central-business side of the organization. I think you'll be generally pleased with how abundant most professionals are when a colleague or even a peer reaches out to draw upon their wisdom.

    - If you work in a smaller business, consider reaching out to the owner or founder to schedule monthly coffee with the intent to understand their vision, the history of the organization, and to even learn from their mistakes and failures (messes) that sharpened their own business insights.

    - Inventory what you are currently reading. Those in marketing should be following sales blogs, magazines, podcasts, and sources that will help them become more familiar with specialized areas. This might include GAAP accounting, Sarbanes Oxley legislation (to understand how the finance division is required to account for revenue and record expenses), or broadening your understanding of Six Sigma and Lean manufacturing processes to better collaborate with operations and your supply chain.

- Invest in and build trusting friendships with other members of your organization so they can faithfully represent you in your absence and keep you updated when your metrics might be off track.

- Memorize and/or print the quote from Albert Einstein and place it somewhere you'll see it often:

"If I had an hour to solve a problem and my life depended on the solution, I would spend the first fifty-five minutes determining the proper question to ask...for once I know the proper question, I could solve the problem in less than five minutes."

CHALLENGE 20

DEVELOP PERSONAS AND THE CUSTOMER JOURNEY

Do you understand the path your current and future buyer is on?

I've deliberately combined two different yet related concepts into this challenge as I've found them to be most useful when interdependently leveraged together: Developing Personas and the Customer Journey.

DEVELOPING PERSONAS

Park City, Utah, is about twenty miles up the mountain from Salt Lake City and is a year-round paradise nobody moves down from—except the Miller family. Our sons were attending school in Salt Lake City, I was commuting to work, and my wife was driving back and forth daily to pick them up. Irritating, especially if your cars are leased. After a year of these annoying commutes, we decided to make a significant lifestyle change and move from a community surrounded by open space and roaming elk, to the heart of the city where the Capitol building is a stone's throw from our backyard. We transitioned from rural life to city life overnight.

During our time in Park City, we joined our community's country club. Yea! It also came bundled with an HOA. Bleh! I know, it's decadent and over the top—trust me, my mother tells me all the time when I take her there for lunch. But hey, I worked very hard for thirty years and this was my reward. You go to Hawaii or buy a sports car; I'll pay my club dues.

Just prior to selling our Park City home, I attended the annual HOA meeting. You know, *the dreaded annual HOA meeting where bored people have nothing to do but complain about embarrassingly trivial problems.* The board had decided to hire a new marketing agency and real estate brokerage to help market the community to prospective buyers. This was a good thing. The community—stunning, safe, and appealing—was increasingly in competition with newer developments attracting second-home buyers and younger successful families with children. There was an amenities war going on and we were losing.

The HOA president introduced the new branding agency to our group of about 150 residents. We clapped politely as they began to unveil their vision for how to present our community to potential buyers. They walked us though some market statistics, acknowledged our brand challenges, and then in an unexpected moment, talked about our community's persona. I thought this was intriguing, given how popular and relevant buyer personas can be for most businesses. I was impressed at their use of the concept, and was interested to see how they would apply it to a residential community.

Then came the slides. As the agency representative began to describe our "community persona," she showed slides of a bicycle in a French countryside of lavender. She went on to share visuals representing our community's lifestyle: a French baguette and a fine glass of Bordeaux all set up for a picnic in the European countryside.

What the hell?

I instantly checked out. She continued, now sounding less decipherable than the muted trombone of Charlie Brown's teacher.

Several minutes later, the presentation came to an end. To the absolute horror of those seated around me, I raised my hand from the back of the room. You could feel the sense of dread as the sound of chairs scooting away from me punctuated the growing sentiment in the room.

Oh crap, Scott Miller has something to say.

Despite this, and to his credit, the board president dutifully called on me. I launched into an incredulous tirade about how idiotic I thought the brand persona was. I demanded to know how a French baguette and a glass of red wine represented our community's brand. Or for that matter, how it helped to market it to potential residents. The agency's pitch of a potential brand persona was more the stuff of an unimaginative European travel brochure than what actually sells homes to up-and-coming young buyers.

I didn't hold back. I said, well, probably way too much.

Okay, admittedly not my best day. At fifty-plus years old, I tend to speak my mind more when I see something is off, but I recognize I could always use more diplomacy (my wife would say *any* would be a start).

Could I have been channeling the frustration that our home had been on the market for nine months with no serious prospects? Sure. But at the heart of my passion was a belief that brand and buyer personas can be extremely valuable—when grounded in reality and filled with more substance than bread. In the case of our community, a better brand persona (and I'll devote one whole minute to thinking about this) might sound like:

> *A private, secluded community set in serene open lands where homeowners of all types can enjoy outdoor beauty and security balanced with superb amenities for every lifestyle.*

It's still a bit vague, I know, but I think buyer personas are more actionable than brand personas. Here are two potential buyer personas for our community:

Jim, the forty-four-year-old tech entrepreneur from California, flush from the recent sale of his company, is looking to move his wife and two teenage kids from the challenges of Southern California to a mountain community with year-round outdoor sports close to an international airport. He reads high-tech, digital magazines, belongs to the YPO (Young Presidents Organization), and likely is an angel investor—or at least knows many who are.

Heather, a fifty-six-year-old plastic surgeon from Dallas with no children, who wants to buy a second ski home for her and her workaholic spouse to both keep her alive and finally begin enjoying the fruits of their labor. They ski annually at Deer Valley and rent their two-week condo through high-end luxury home sites.

You'll notice no baguettes, no Bordeaux, and no lavender fields— less fluff and more stuff. And that stuff is based on data already known about our residents, our competition, and what makes our community the obvious choice among many others. Buyer personas are absolutely crucial to understanding who is buying from us now and, thus, who should be in the future. But they can be useless if they're just creative caricatures based more on poetic writing and stock photos than facts. Such flights of fancy rarely result in any revenue-generating activity.

The mess that faces marketers is a failure to craft your brand or buyer personas accurately and based on data. The fact of the matter is I'm a fairly sophisticated person, but I've never been in a lavender field riding a bicycle or quaffed a glass of Bordeaux. Baguettes, however? My main source of nutrition. You get the point: manufacturing your ideal buyer is a vastly different exercise than creating a legitimate buyer persona. Put your ego aside, sharpen your pencil, and get factual and real about who your target market is. It's the only way a brand or buyer persona will ever add any value to your marketing initiatives.

As far as the HOA meeting at the beginning of the challenge goes, you may be wondering if my eloquent and well-thought-out soliloquy changed anything. The truth is, I have no idea. I slinked out the back door, clearly *persona non grata*. I think the big lesson to be learned here is that when you're tempted to develop brand and buyer personas, be certain they are both based on data and are actionable, and that they're not feel-good fluff that may make for a nice PowerPoint presentation but isn't going to materially impact your marketing strategy. Another lesson to keep in mind is that just because you're working for a branding or marketing agency doesn't guarantee you're an expert in either.

THE CUSTOMER JOURNEY

Similar to personas, your customer journeys must be based as much on fact as possible and are only as valuable as they are accurate and grounded in reality. To think otherwise is a marketing mess in the waiting.

A customer's journey is simply their entire experience with you. From beginning to, well, not the end. Ideally, there never is an end. Some marketing teams map the customer journey to buyer personas. Actual buying clients are sometimes profiled or replicated as "look-alikes" because they are very similar to those already in the fold. The potential marketing mess with look-alikes is that they're often based on correlational data—they're similar to other people on "paper," but often very different in circumstance. For example, couples in their seventies selling their homes in a certain ZIP code may seem similar from a data-set perspective, but in reality can be in completely different circumstances. It would be risky to assume such couples are all downsizing to move into senior-only communities. Many, in fact, may be motivated by reasons as diverse as health, freedom, peace of mind, proximity to family, etc.

Renowned professor Clayton Christensen and consultant Bob Moesta popularized the term "Job to Be Done," now adopted by companies globally as a lens for innovation. By now we've all heard the quote by Harvard marketing professor Theodore Levitt: "People don't want to buy a quarter-inch drill. They want a quarter-inch hole" (what they really want is to hang their new flat-screen TV on the wall without it falling off). Are you clear on why your clients are investing with you? What "job" are they hiring you to solve? Clayton writes extensively about the value of diving deep into understanding what exact circumstance your customer is in when they begin searching for your solution. Wedding planning? Death of a pet? Need a larger vehicle to accommodate a growing family? Rapid business growth and explosive onboarding of new employees? Completing a merger and facing the inevitable culture clash? Experiencing a trust scandal in the C-suite with a regulatory intervention imminent?

You get the idea. Increasingly known as circumstance-based marketing, the clearer you are on a client's specific circumstance—what they're facing or the issue or problem they need to solve—the closer your customer journey can be to reality; also, the more prepared you are to communicate directly with them and move them swiftly though your marketing and sales funnel.

It's embarrassing how many of us never determined what circumstance our buyers were in when we designed our offerings and products. It's a mess we often find ourselves in late in the design process, or more likely, even post-launch (remember the Roomba lesson from Challenge 10?) It's never too late to become more precise in our understanding of the varied circumstances we should be addressing. Assign someone to interview your current clients and listen for the nuggets that help you understand their journey. Do this once, with as many clients as possible, becoming obsessive about understanding the precise circumstances your customers are in when they're purchasing your products or services.

Be careful, however, as there's a potential marketing mess in abdicating this responsibility to the secondhand perspective of the sales representative. I've been humbled too many times by the following: I'll be trying to collect data on the main circumstances our buyers are in, and first call the frontline sales professional who managed and closed the deal. They will recap the lineage of the client's journey and do so with extreme confidence in their accuracy. Then I will talk directly with the client and be stunned at the disparity between how the client saw their journey versus how the sales associate did. Rarely did we plot the early, pivotal points accurately. So heed this warning: Validate your internal lessons with direct client interviews to ensure you're building journeys that are true to life and not fiction. Here are some thoughts to consider as you build your customer-journey maps:

- Which and how many specific circumstances have you determined your buyers are in?

- Can you narrow them to the largest segments and afford to ignore the fractured subsegments?

- How specific can you get on the key decision points along their journey? Are you able to elevate some above others that are naturally more important to be present for? How early can you meet buyers in their journey so you're top of mind? Is that wise, or should a competitor do that work for you (like spending the time, effort, and money to educate the health-food consumer on the benefits of kombucha versus you just swooping in at the end and competing on price)? This is a bet you must make about precisely when you would like to become part of the customer's journey.

- Have you paid the price to validate how you address their key decision points along the journey so you aren't wasting any time or assets guessing? Groupthink in marketing can be your worst enemy. Become very comfortable asking, "How do we know that? Have we asked the client that question?"

FROM MESS TO SUCCESS:

DEVELOP PERSONAS AND THE CUSTOMER JOURNEY

- Read every article, blog, and book, and listen to every speech you can find from Clayton Christensen. Of his many profound ideas, the concept of knowing your customers' circumstance is perhaps the most valuable marketing insight you can focus on (tied with smallest viable market from Seth Godin).

- Give yourself ample time to research, validate, and align with the circumstances of your ideal client.

  - Consistently challenge your findings by asking, "How do we *know* that?"

  - When you've become clear on what circumstance they're in while searching for a solution, you can align every marketing investment and activity with that circumstance.

- Remember the adage: *People don't want to buy a quarter-inch drill. They want a quarter-inch hole. For their television. So they can sit on their sofa with a beer and watch professional wrestling.* What is your customer's equivalent to the six-inch hole?

- Base your brand and buyer personas in reality.

CHALLENGE 21

SPEAK THEIR
LANGUAGE

*Are you conversant in the language of your
customer, or stuck with your native tongue?*

The 7 Habits of Highly Effective People is one of the bestselling books in history. In print for over thirty years, it's sold forty million copies and has been translated into over fifty languages. As impactful as the book is to read, the live program is life-changing and the most widely offered personal and professional development program available to organizations worldwide. Millions of professionals have attended this program, and it's as relevant today as when Dr. Covey wrote it at the age of fifty-six (so there's still time for you and me to do something equally impactful).

Every five to seven years, our company updates the actual program to ensure it's current, with fresh examples, videos, exercises, tools, and for our high-tech clients, a participant kit either in print or digital that meets their needs. At FranklinCovey, our Innovations division typically owns the designing of new offerings, the Marketing division launches them, and Sales, well, as you know by my opening chapters, pays all our salaries by crushing it with our valued clients.

Several years ago, the latest version of our *7 Habits* work session was on the cusp of completion and, as the CMO, I was responsible for the global launch, supported by our entire team. We developed ambitious plans for the campaign (to many people's annoyance, I'm incapable of being anything less than "ambitious" in every project I touch).

Complementing the many launch activities, we ended up with a 177-city world tour wherein we showcased the new offering to buyers in over fifty countries. These were three-hour live events in which human resource leaders, chief learning officers, business-unit leaders, and anyone responsible for the training and development of their employees could preview the new work session. It was a massive effort. I'd liken it to hosting 177 weddings in 90 days. For the most part, the event followed an established formula except for localization for customs and language. We hosted events—many on the same day—in cities like Stockholm, Madrid, Auckland, Baghdad, Buenos Aires, Tulsa, and St. Louis. It was not uncommon to have fifteen to twenty events happening simultaneously, and as a result, we had what seemed to be an open line to UPS and FedEx as we tracked missing or late shipments. We even flew a colleague to Sydney, Australia, to deliver six suitcases of event materials, only to return that person the very next day, as it was cheaper than shipping the materials via UPS. Yes, this colleague was tired, but they loved the air miles.

The event was a massive success for both our clients and our brand. We substantially exceeded our revenue goals as our team worked tirelessly to execute the campaign. Congratulations to them are definitely in order!

The planning for this global launch was nearly twelve months long. Coordinating the logistics around 177 live events required venue scheduling, consultant selection, and training- and participant-material development. Presentations needed to be designed and redesigned many times until test audiences found it compelling enough to make a purchase.

Additionally, we had to create extensive marketing to populate all the events. We needed a registration system, email templates, landing pages, and confirmation and cancellation procedures for the countless registrations coming and going by the minute. Then there was direct mail and collateral for the salespeople in the field to use at face-to-face meetings. In fact, as I type this, I find I'm a bit nostalgic and incredulous that we pulled it all off so well.

Every participant needed three to four months' notice to hold the date. So that meant you're marketing an event without a complete solution to sell, so no finalized messaging or materials are available. You're checking in daily (hourly) with the product designers to understand any changes they're making to ensure your messaging and positioning is accurate and compelling. It's a test of confidence and courage, and as my dad would say, one that "separates the boys from the men." No gender prejudice intended.

So where's the mess you ask? Don't worry, it's coming.

Midway into designing the flow of the event and the entire global launch, the company hired a marketing associate to help the leadership division at FranklinCovey. Jessica Johnson was not part of the formal marketing team (meaning she wasn't interviewed or hired by me and didn't report to me). We naturally invited her into the launch meetings, albeit with some trepidation. Her role was to support the leadership vertical market for our company, and we needed to collaborate as she was becoming responsible for the *7 Habits* brand. Note I chose the word *needed*, not *wanted*. She seemed pleasant enough, and although she had a strong marketing background, none of it was in our field or industry.

During her first week on the job, I sat in a design meeting with her, talking through the script our consultants would learn when presenting the event. We always develop a script, then once the consultant passes the test to qualify for the event, they can customize it to their own comfort level. This obviously has both upsides and downsides—you don't want rote, memorized delivery, but you also don't want consultants "going off the ranch."

As I finished presenting a whole section of the first hour of the event, I looked at this new associate, expecting her to be in awe of my eloquence and affirm that she was in the presence of genius.

Nope, that ain't what happened.

With uncharacteristic boldness for our culture (she was new, mind you, so she didn't fully appreciate my need to be deferred to), she said, "I have no idea what most of that meant. Nobody talks that way."

BOOM!

I looked at her, speechless (which doesn't happen often). I sat down, hating her, and listened. She went on to talk about how confusing much of our internal language was and argued that none of the people in any of her previous companies referred to the situations/problems/issues/ events with the same nomenclature. She didn't pull any punches. She wasn't rude or insulting, just clear and convincing.

On that day, I came to realize the absurd vernacular our corporate language had morphed into. I was using terms like "stewardship" to describe "responsibilities." She asked, "Is that some sort of church term?" She wasn't kidding. Other terms, which seemed very normal to me because we'd said them thousands of times in meetings, had now made their way into our public-facing messages.

We kind of stared at each other for a few seconds as I thought, *I still don't really like her, but she's absolutely right*. From that instant forward, we reassessed every word, description, scenario, exercise, or anything else that might be embedded with our internal language. The team asked for her opinion often, and while she had zero expertise in our business or market positioning, she was invaluable in calling BS on our hoity-toity language and self-referencing terms. We made changes across the board. As a result of her feedback, we discovered we were in a marketing mess of our own making. And there's a good chance you're doing the same thing in your organization.

Don't believe me? It's more likely to happen than you think.

A decade earlier, I had recently returned to the United States from an assignment in the United Kingdom and had invited three British colleagues to a winter ski vacation at my little cabin in Park City. We had a blast skiing and telling horror stories about the American (me) who landed in the UK and how they chewed him up and spat him out. One day on the slopes, they took me aside and told me I was talking business all day, even while we were skiing. I protested and asked what they meant— to the best of my recollection, I hadn't brought up work during a single conversation that day. My visitors explained that FranklinCovey's terms had so penetrated my natural vocabulary that they couldn't tell when I was on personal time and when I was working. One of them, a dear friend to this day named Esther Flatley, announced, "Scott, do you know how many times this week you've told me you're 'just trying to add value'? Who says that outside of work?" She went on to share her wonder at my ability to work "synergy" into our lunch conversation, reminding me that she also worked for the same company and needed a break.

We all laughed (I was horrified), but I became much more aware of my language after that vacation. Or did I? Sadly it was ten years after I'd received the tough feedback from my British friends that Jessica had the same intervention with me during the *7 Habits* launch meeting. Entrenched habits are hard to break, but in marketing, language is at the heart of what we do. So avoid the mess and be more mindful if you're speaking *your* language or your *client's*.

By no means is this a cultural issue unique to FranklinCovey. Every organization is rife with their own nomenclature, short cuts, acronyms, and internal language that undoubtedly works its way into your value proposition, external marketing messages, sales training, and overall advertising and business-development investments. Self-awareness about your internally referenced language does not come easy. As a marketer, you will need to continually develop a cadence to meet with clients, nonclients, and even individuals outside your industry to continually benchmark and field-test to ensure that what you're calling *it* is also what they're calling *it*. And further, that what they're calling *it* is also what's budgeted for as a problem to be solved. You might be selling productivity software that solves a project-management issue to a potential client who is actually funded under a leadership-development category, but who really aligns with an overall company goal of increasing their speed to market. Connecting these four dots is all on the back of the language your sales and marketing team is speaking, or perhaps more importantly, listening for. It's another reason why understanding the circumstance your buyer is in is so vital, because different circumstances typically align with different terms and languages (even when you're convinced that you're speaking the same language).

FROM MESS TO SUCCESS:

SPEAK THEIR LANGUAGE

- Become trilingual: know your language, that of your business/industry/culture, and what's actually spoken by your customer. The more you directly interact with current clients and prospects, the better you will become at speaking in the customer's vernacular.

  - Search LinkedIn and connect to a few potential (but not current buyers).

  - Ask them if you could take fifteen minutes to learn from them.

  - Consider declaring upfront: "I wonder if you'd be willing to invest fifteen minutes with me as I am trying to better understand some specific circumstances our clients are in when they choose to use our products and services. I know you're not a current client, and my intent is not to try to make you one on this call. I simply wondered if you might answer some questions for me as we continue to refine our messaging to ensure it's on point and helps to solve our buyer's needs." Customize the script as needed and honor the fifteen-minute time parameter. If someone sent me that request, honored the time commitment, and didn't try to sell to me on the call, I'd absolutely throw them a quarter of an hour.

- Conduct a top-of-mind brainstorm and write out all the words you use consistently inside your company.

  - Ask a colleague to join you and have some fun with it.

  - When you're sure your list is comprehensive, sit back and reflect on it. Email it to a few trusted clients and ask them to highlight or circle any words they use in their own day-to-day dealings but which did not arise as a result of working with you (you don't want to taint the jury pool).

You may be shocked at how few matches there are.

- Take a nonclient acquaintance for a quick coffee and ask them to validate or challenge how close your conversation is to their real, day-to-day conversations.

  - Work to understand how proximate your marketing language is to your clients' real-life challenges.

  - Recognize that what you call "high performance," someone else may call "best in class." Those terms mean very different things, and one's marketing strategy would be fundamentally different based on which conversation *they* were trying to engage in.

CHALLENGE 22

BUILD LISTS
THAT MATTER

*Is your creative genius and irresistible offer
being messaged to the right people?*

A seasoned marketing leader once taught me that effective campaigns are based one-third each on the quality of the creative, the quality of the offer, and the quality of the list. This has stayed with me through literally hundreds of different initiatives.

My experience now would reorder it as 60 percent list, 20 percent offer, and 20 percent creative—which sucks, because the creative part is the most fun for many marketing teams. The bottom line is you may have the most compelling and creative offer, but if you're aimed at the wrong prospect, it's a complete waste of everyone's time and effort. Your list is paramount to any campaign. Everything in your strategy can be world-class in quality and execution, but if your list blows, you're just *spraying and praying*—an idiom from the military about the amateurish use of automatic weapons on the battlefield.

Ask yourself whether you're net fishing or spear fishing. Chris McChesney, the lead author of the number-one *Wall Street Journal* bestseller *The 4 Disciplines of Execution*, popularized this idea with respect to finding prospects. Net fishing is casting a large net across the water and scooping up a huge bounty that includes lobsters, groupers, eels, catfish, a few tires, buoys, and some seaweed. All fine if you're opening an ocean-themed restaurant and need both ingredients for the kitchen and decoration for the walls. Spear fishing entails knowing exactly where the flounder feed and using a spear to stab one after another. Okay, a bit macabre, but you end up with a cooler full of exactly what you planned to grill.

List-building requires patience, care, and deliberation often beyond reason. In the above analogy, it's about using a spear. It takes longer than a net, requires greater skill, and can be fatiguing as you take the boat back and forth. But your list of prospects will likely be in the ideal circumstance to resonate with your message.

Case in point: Several years ago, the mailroom delivered a large box to my office. It was about three by four feet and likely weighed fifteen pounds. I receive lots of direct mail and packages as a senior leader and am the beneficiary of many "get your attention" deliveries. This includes View-Masters, golf balls, cupcakes, and calendars—they all go you know where. This one was very different, however. Far too big for the garbage can (obviously, part of their strategy).

As I opened the brown shipping box with a UK return address, my interest piqued. Inside was a stunning mahogany box, polished perfectly, with my name on a gold plate. I opened it and found a customized collection of sports paraphernalia supporting a popular English football team, including a custom team jersey with MILLER embroidered on the back. Beneath a team-themed scarf, I found a certificate authenticating both, along with an invitation to sponsor their team. I can't do justice to the beauty of this box and its contents here. The investment in this promotion, door to door, must have been more than five hundred dollars. My response was one of being both honored and perplexed.

Why me? Why FranklinCovey? I couldn't figure out why a well-known British football team would target an American, in Salt Lake City, working in leadership development, as a potential sponsor. We certainly didn't have a history of doing this, or for that matter, really any significant sponsorships outside of some underprivileged schools. Our UK business, although solid, certainly wasn't large enough to warrant this level of spend. And then there's me—you can easily find my name and contact information, but even a cursory look at my many social platforms would tell you European football is not on the list of things I pay any attention to. I'm guessing they had reasons for identifying me/us as a legitimate opportunity, but the truth is I'll never know. Why? *Because they never even followed up on their five-hundred-dollar box.* No calls, no emails, no voicemails, no LinkedIn messages, no nothing. This is a textbook case of *what not to do*: Amazingly creative. Solid and clear offer. But I was the rusted bicycle caught in a net aimed at bluefin tuna.

But the story didn't end there. A few days later, during the weekly Monday executive team meeting, the CEO brought to the conference table, where his team was seated, a perfectly polished mahogany box with *his* name on a gold plate. He withdrew the customized team jersey with WHITMAN embroidered on the back, along with all the same accoutrements. He was quite impressed at its opulence, but admitted, "It seems strange they targeted me for this. And further, they never even followed up." He looked over at me and I commented on what an honor it was for him to have received it—and said nothing else.

What I was thinking however was: *Make that a thousand-dollar investment.*

The most logical answer to me for all of this is that some Qatari sheikh had a million dollars to blow on promoting sponsorships for his pet-project football team. Either that, or total incompetence on the part of the team's marketing division. They clearly didn't vet their list. Or even build it. Or look at it. They likely hired some list broker to find American companies of a certain size or profile, and crossed their fingers that we were in the market to sponsor a UK football team. To clarify, this would not have been our circumstance. Not even close. All would have been fine, I guess, had it been a letter or even a nicely printed invitation. Three to four dollars at the most. But a custom jersey with my name on it? Carefully folded into a hand-carved burled-wood box? Shipped halfway around the world?

Listen to me: Carefully curate your list. Throw spears instead of casting nets. Ask yourself, "What is the circumstance a client needs to be in to buy or sponsor our product or service?" Is it a merger, an acquisition, technology integration, litigation, downturn in revenue, massive expansion, supply-chain or vendor issues, legislative mandates, or something else? How do I know this information is accurate? Have I invested the time and focus to locate the right people in the right circumstance?

Most organizations put massive energy and attention into all sorts of research and analysis, but they then farm out building their databases to third-party sources who are selling the same tired lists to all their competitors. These lists atrophy 30 percent a year, which means every thirty-six months, the data is basically useless. I have used every list broker in the business and they all have generally the same data. One exception I've found is a firm located in South Florida called Worldata. I've worked with them for nearly a decade and I really value their data and service. The CEO, Jay Schwedelson, is a trusted advisor to FranklinCovey on a variety of data and digital needs and has become a personal friend.

I truly respect Jay's guidance and the advice from the colleagues in his firm. Check them out at Worldata.com.

To complement our work with Worldata, I led a highly unconventional old-school list-building effort that I learned in my early days working on numerous political campaigns, and further refined during my years at the Disney Development Company. We needed to acquire clean and evergreen data on our prospects, and found the best way to maintain the initiative was to roll up our sleeves, research it, and compile it ourselves. I know, beyond belief in 2021. We hired a group of part-time researchers that included college students, stay-at-home parents, and former employees looking to pick up a few hours. We also built a full-time team of four individuals whose sole job was to be on the internet all day researching and confirming highly targeted, new names for our database. Not just names, but completely verified records including titles, physical mailing addresses, phone numbers, email addresses, and social media handles. Information was cross-referenced via LinkedIn, Google, company websites, association member lists, and many other proprietary methods that resulted in a world-class list with highly accurate data. Again, we choose to throw a spear a lot instead of casting a few nets. Then our lists were segmented by every possible circumstance and matched to which Job to Be Done they may be facing and which of our solutions was a likely fit. There was some guessing of course, but the spear was sharp!

We became so adept at filling our marketing events and webcasts that we routinely closed them and, unfortunately, turned people away. Further, our data quality and capacity often outpaced our strategy to deploy it.

Stop the mess of frivolously buying and blind-renting data to spray out your message. Instead, pull out your spear, determine your smallest viable market, and build some perfect lists yourself. You will be amazed at the results. It's a highly labor-intensive effort when done well, but the payoff is absolutely worth it—especially when you actually follow up.

FROM MESS TO SUCCESS:

BUILD LISTS THAT MATTER

- Recognize that you may need to subordinate your own creative desires to the vital activity of building and maintaining your lists.

  - Ensure the veracity of your list. Do your best to confirm it, then raise your standard and confirm again. This is not a one-and-done event, but an ongoing activity. This is often referred to in the industry as "list hygiene."

  - When you're developing a campaign aimed at new prospects, focus an inordinate amount of energy and time on your list. A great standard is "Measure twice, cut once." Be sure you know exactly what data you will eventually need so you collect it on the front end. It's painful and expensive to realize you should have also collected email addresses while you were researching physical mailing addresses. Or you've built a massive database of physical corporate mailing addresses—and I know this is outrageously unthinkable, but imagine for a moment that a global pandemic hits and everyone begins working virtually from home, thus rendering your list useless for any kind of direct-mail campaign. Impossible, right? Think carefully about what you need up front.

  - Only after your list is complete should you begin the creative parts of your campaign, or have them run concurrently but minimally, and recognize that one is clearly more fun than the other, so calibrate your resources and attention accordingly.

- Develop a point of view of whom you're targeting:

  - From what sources, and how, will you curate your list?

  - Will your list be segmented based on different circumstances or other psychographics?

- What is your process for obtaining and maintaining accurate contact information on your targeted suspects?

- Are you net fishing or spearfishing? I am never hungry enough to eat the occasional eel caught in the lobster net. Whomever your target is, go to where they are and aim carefully. It may take more practice than your current level of patience offers, but it is always quality over quantity when it comes to your list. To remind you, more is not better; better is better.

CHALLENGE 23

LEVERAGE YOUR PROMOTERS

*What are you doing to support and
motivate your raving fans?*

Chick-fil-A is one of the premiere examples in American business of how to best leverage your promoters. If the name of the restaurant elicits a strong emotional response—be it either for the love of their food or, for others, a disagreement with the founder's religious beliefs and politics—try to put it aside for a moment, because the point I'm going to share is important and worthy of your consideration.

Chick-fil-A is one of the most profitable fast-food chains in history. Its per-store revenue and profit far exceed every one of its competitors—by a lot. I recently interviewed Donald Miller, a consultant to Chick-fil-A and author of the bestselling book *Building a Story Brand.* He shared that one of the chain's biggest challenges is they can't build onsite freezers at their stores large enough to hold all the chicken they're going to sell that day. What a great problem to have. When is the last time you've heard of a business that can't inventory enough product to meet their clients' needs? *On a daily basis!* During the early days of the global 2020 pandemic, at least in Salt Lake City, the Chick-fil-A drive-thrus were a hundred cars deep morning and night, as the physical restaurant itself was closed to walk-in traffic.

As a private company, they have policies some detractors are fiercely opposed to. Occasionally, small gatherings have been organized in restaurant parking lots to protest the founder's personal views on social matters and the company's policies and political contributions. I have no dog in this hunt; my point in sharing it is what typically happens next.

It seems that within minutes of protesters assembling, Chick-fil-A customers, whatever their own agenda may be, come calling by the hundreds (if not thousands). The lines are soon out the door, and the cars in the drive-thru stretch for blocks. I have no idea if the antiprotesters (Chick-fil-A promoters) care about defending the company's policies and the right to freedom of speech as a private enterprise, or if they just have a hankering for a chicken sandwich and don't want to see their favorite restaurant harmed. I imagine all types are present.

The point is, this business clearly has rabid promoters that can drown out the detractors. I suspect there's no secret text brigade or silent whistle to bring on the cavalry. Protesters show up and then so do the supporters.

The news story almost always shifts from the protest group to the sight of legions of customers clogging the drive-thru for hours. Chick-fil-A has built an army of customers, in forty-seven states who, on their own volition, come to their aid whenever and wherever they need them to—without even asking. And don't forget the small fact that these promoters buy more chicken than the stores can warehouse onsite.

How did Chick-fil-A get such a faithful following? That's the multimillion-dollar question, and there are probably more answers than I can write in this book. You will have your own opinion, based on whether you're a promoter or detractor, but the company is clearly doing a lot of things right to build such a loyal customer base. Here's one thing I think everyone can agree upon: they treat their employees exceedingly well and, as a result, the employees treat the customers exceedingly well. This is a timeless business principle Chick-fil-A has nailed, and it has resulted in nearly unparalleled franchisee retention (96 percent, according to a recent article)[14] and palpable loyalty from their promoting customers.

Your promoters are your brand ambassadors and de facto salespeople, so what is your strategy to nurture and leverage them? Here are some questions to ask your marketing team to ensure your promoters can rival Chick-fil-A's:

- Who are your current promoters and are they encouraged to continue promoting your business? Are you giving them specific reasons, experiences, and lasting impressions to motivate them to act independently on your behalf?

- Are you aware of why they consider themselves promoters? Was there a defining event with your product and service that, if you knew about it, you would make sure every other client had the same experience?

---

14 Kruse, Kevin (2015) "How Chick-fil-A Created a Culture That Lasts," *Forbes*, 8 Dec. Available from https://www.forbes.com/sites/kevinkruse/2015/12/08/how-chick-fil-a-created-a-culture-that-lasts/#505370a33602.

- What do you know about them? Do you keep and maintain contact information for them without violating their desire to just buy your product or service and not have to sign up to become your new, lifelong digital BFF?

- What data-hygiene processes do you have in place to ensure you're up to date on how to connect with them in ways they prefer?

- If you sell services through them to their organization and they change employers, do you know it and have a process to make it easy for them to "take you with them"?

- How often do you communicate to and with them, and does this add any value for them?

- Do you have easy feedback mechanisms in place for them, specifically so they can help you "right any perceived wrongs" they see?

- Do you help to responsibly shape their narrative about your brand? If needed, do they have real-time access to your company's position on issues and trends?

- Perhaps they're strong supporters of a particular product, but you need them to promote your latest launch. What bridge are you building for them from Product A to Product B?

- What incentives, if any, are in place to encourage them to promote and refer other clients or customers?

As important as these previous points are for your reflection—and hopefully action—admittedly, they're somewhat self-serving. To build and leverage your promoters, you must be certain not to remain internally focused only on *your* needs, but tip the balance toward *theirs*. My experience is that many of us marketers are so driven and fixated on landing new customers that we often neglect those who came around early, believed in us, and stuck with us, even when we didn't fully earn or deserve it. Does this describe your business at all? It certainly describes the mobile-phone business. Everyone knows the big secret: the longer you've been with a provider, the more you pay. We get so focused on the potential mess around what's next and who's next that we lose touch with the timeless adage "Dance with the one who brung you." Which means (if you're too young to have heard this one) be loyal to those who believed in and cherished you first.

Here are some additional thoughts to consider:

- How often do you thank your customers? When was the last time someone senior in your organization, beyond the client-facing salesperson, reached out to a customer and thanked them?

- If you do have a process for thanking your customers, does it come with baggage? Is your thank-you always wrapped in an offer to buy more, or does it come with a discount on their next purchase? When was the last time you thanked your customers, no strings attached?

- What would it look like if you created an initiative to do so? Could it expand their loyalty and your business? Could your referrals grow?

- New-customer acquisition is a common focus and measure in many organizations. We rarely hear or see the same level of focus about retention unless it's a subscription-based business, and then it's an obsessive measure. Beyond that, it seems to get executive lip service, but I think, overall, it's undercommunicated, underfunded, and undernurtured.

Recently I was in a restaurant, and as I left, I thanked the host. Their response was, "You're welcome." *What? You're Welcome* for letting me spend my money at your restaurant? *You're Welcome* for allowing me to eat here? *Are you kidding?* What they should have said was, "It was our pleasure. Thank you for your business; we're honored you joined us and please come back." But this never happens. To take it a step further, the customer should not be initiating an exit (or entry) conversation with any seller.

Here's a perfect example of this principle illustrated in a positive light. As I mentioned, two years ago, I moved twenty miles down the mountain from Park City to Salt Lake City; yet, I still drive the twenty miles back up, twice a month, to get my hair cut at the same salon I've been with for ten years running. To be honest, a man's haircut is a man's haircut. I'm sure there's an abundance of eminently qualified hair stylists within blocks of my home. Yet, I continue, twice monthly, driving up to Park City because of the way the owner treats me. Not only does Jake accommodate all of my last-minute ambush appointment requests, he thanks me for my business at every appointment and, as he waits for me to pay my bill at the counter, stands by the front door and opens it for me as I leave (as he does for every customer). Each time without fail. Jake Robbins is the co-owner/principal of Lit Salon and is going to have to fire me because I ain't quitting him—and that's not an ode to *Brokeback Mountain*.

No business has a right to exist (especially vaping stores, because I have three small boys and this is my book). Every business must earn and reearn that right every day. If I owned a restaurant, I would walk up to every table (at some appropriate time) and genuinely thank the customers for their business. I would say, "I hope you enjoyed your meal. I want to personally thank you for spending your money with us. I am grateful for your business. I look forward to seeing you again." I am not exaggerating here. This simple effort would drive insane repeat business. The same would happen if I owned a retail store, or for that matter, any type of business. As an officer in our company, whenever I am on the phone with a client (usually during a pre-consult for a speech they've hired me for), I always thank them for their business first. I purposefully slow down and change the pacing of the conversation so they can genuinely feel my appreciation for their business with our company. I think it's a lost courtesy, especially in the B2B market.

I was at a tennis store recently in Salt Lake City and spent $350 on equipment for my boys. The owner was at the cash register and, after I paid (in cash), I said, "Thank you." She didn't even look up at me, and her response was—and I am not making this up—"Uh-huh." Do you think I will ever shop in that store again? You know the answer. And you can be assured not only am I *not* a promoter of her business, I will vocally deter people from shopping there. In the current economy, no customer can be taken for granted.

Why am I schooling you on customer service in a marketing book? Because how you treat your promoters *is* marketing. For good or bad. And those who learn to leverage their promoters will always have the advantage (tennis pun intended).

Ever heard of the Baader-Meinhof phenomenon? Maybe not, but you've surely lived it. You bought a new brand of car you rarely saw on the road before, and now you see it everywhere. This happens in all areas of our life: products, phrases, brands, etc. The more you are aware of something, the more you start seeing and recognizing it. I'll bet the same thing happens to you after reading this chapter: the next time someone says, "You're welcome," you'll be wondering if they should have said, "Thank you," instead. But more importantly, you'll be cognizant of your own thanking behavior when it comes to your customers and promoters.

FROM MESS TO SUCCESS:

LEVERAGE YOUR PROMOTERS

- Evaluate the balance between maintaining your current clients' engagement and the need for targeting new opportunities.

  - Have you acknowledged whether the thrill of the hunt is hurting your need to nurture?

- Recognize that we all have natural predispositions to be easily distracted, so build momentum with new challenges and new opportunities.

  - What will you do to ensure you set goals and achieve them as they relate to engaging, tracking, following, and remagnetizing your buyers when they tire, get distracted, or require a reminder of why they were clients in the first place?

- Research competitors in your industry, especially those who might be eating your lunch.

  - Why are their fans raving? spending? staying?

  - What can you learn from them to build your own promoters?

CHALLENGE 24

THE RESPONSIBLE
RESURGENCE OF PRINT

In the cyclone of digital communications,
is print a timely complement?

For my entire life, the United States Postal Service has delivered mail to my home, except for a few years when I had a PO Box instead. I've lived in Florida, Illinois, and Utah, and these mail deliveries typically came around eleven o'clock but never any later than three o'clock. Starting about a year ago, the mail at my home in Salt Lake City began showing up around six or seven o'clock. I noticed it immediately, because a mail carrier walking around in the dark is an odd, even somewhat unsettling sight. Several times over the past month, I've stopped the postal workers (increasingly in my neighborhood, it's not always the same person) and gently inquired why they were working into the evening. All of their responses amounted to the same thing: more mail to deliver. So much so, that it's forcing the carriers to work longer just to get it all done. And it's not just Amazon packages, but normal, old-fashioned mail: birthday cards, coupons, offers from car dealerships, lawn services, real estate announcements, credit card bills, bank statements, community newsletters, etc. My mail in 2020 hasn't lessened from ten years ago, amounting to five to seven pieces a day, and that's not including the numerous packages from various retailers my wife deftly unboxes and integrates into our home while I'm distracted. It's still endearing to me that she thinks I don't know this is how she spends part of her afternoons. And by the way, the same thing's happening at your house, but perhaps the roles are reversed.

DISCLAIMER: THIS CHALLENGE WAS ORIGINALLY WRITTEN PRIOR TO THE GLOBAL COVID-19 IMPACT ON IN-PERSON GATHERINGS AND THE NECESSITY OF SOCIAL DISTANCING, WHICH ELIMINATED MOST LIVE EVENTS. I'VE INTENTIONALLY LEFT THIS CHAPTER IN, AS LIVE EVENTS WILL ONCE AGAIN BECOME A STANDARD WAY OF DOING BUSINESS, ALBEIT WITH NEW SAFETY PRACTICES OR LESSONS IN PLACE. THE MARKETING PRACTICES I OUTLINE HERE RELATED TO DIRECT MAIL ARE PERHAPS EVEN MORE RELEVANT WHEN THE WORLD RETURNS TO SOME DEGREE OF POST-VACCINE NORMALCY.

MARKETING MESS TO BRAND SUCCESS

All this mail continues to accumulate despite the fact that most of our bills are on autopay and we choose digital statements when available. I'm on many do-not-mail lists and rarely sign up for anything new in print. And yet, the daily deluge persists. Why? Take a moment to consider your own email inbox. Mine has pretty much exploded. I receive about three hundred emails a day, the vast majority of which are solicitations I never even see as they're automatically moved to clutter and junk folders. I marvel at the hundreds if not thousands of emails waiting in electronic purgatory for my assistant to pass judgment on and send into the abyss, unopened and unread. Corporate email filters have never been tighter, be they human or digital.

The truth is, people are more likely to look through printed mail than email, assuming that email even manages to make its way through the filters standing in the way. Research from the United States Postal Service even found that 84 percent of millennials, as tech-savvy as they are, take the time necessary to look through their traditional mail. So much so that 64 percent of them would rather scan for useful information in their printed mail than in email.[15]

The onslaught of unsolicited email, texts, and social posts has certainly hit a tipping point in my life, and is likely why the printed medium still holds such an appeal. This is compounded by the explosion of marketing automation services, whereby organizations load up a series of algorithmically segmented outbound emails, only to be followed by a series of responses based on your open, click, or engagement rate. And increasingly, these automated emails are written in such a casual manner as to manipulate you into feeling that this person knows you. The main reason I don't open 95 percent of my email is that it's likely automated. I could also write an entire chapter on the explosion of social media channels and chatbots allowing for alternate communication

---

15   Vinnedge, Phil (2016) *USPS Mail Moments: 2016 Review*, March. Available from: https://tensionenvelope.com/sites/default/files/2016_mail_moments_report_may_160504_1400.pdf?_ga=2.58198946.908866539.1605551921-847786671605551921.

mechanisms. My LinkedIn inbox is now officially larger than my Outlook inbox.

These new technology mediums provide an interesting opportunity for responsible direct mail. Here's an example from my own career, when a carefully designed direct-mail piece successfully infiltrated the otherwise impenetrable inboxes of the C-suite (and not just once, but repeatedly).

Pre-COVID, FranklinCovey hosted hundreds of live in-person events around the nation annually—substantially more when you factor in our fifty-plus offices around the world. A common refrain in our company is "Nothing sells FranklinCovey like a FranklinCovey experience." When business leaders joined us for a breakfast or lunch event hosted at a local hotel or even at a client site, something magical happened. We didn't need to sell anything. If we simply taught from our leadership content, most participants saw the value of partnering with us to transform their leaders and cultures. And we weren't alone; any hotel would have been hosting many similar events with organizations from across a variety of industries to showcase their respective talents and offerings. Live in-person marketing events are as robust and relevant today as they were twenty years ago, recognizing that currently, the vast majority are being done virtually. At some point, these live in-person events will reemerge. As an alternative, FranklinCovey now likely hosts more webcasts and podcasts than any organization in the nation—perhaps the world.

Which begs the question: How do you get decision-making prospective clients to register and actually show up? This is the difficult part. Increasingly, the amount of time a prospect has to spend at one of our events is inversely correlated with their level of decision making— *those* folks are planning out the severance packages for everyone who has time to go off-site and attend a lunch. Of course, this is a bit hyperbolic, but there's also some truth in it. Everyone is overbooked, overburdened, and overworked—especially those at the more senior levels. It's sadly the new norm that senior leaders rarely take time to invest in their own learning and development. Getting their attention is nearly impossible.

Or is it?

FranklinCovey hosts an invite-only series of events aimed squarely at the C-suite. We don't typically publish them on our website and we're quite deliberate about the seniority of the participants. That's not meant to be discriminatory, as we have a full slate of events for professionals at all levels. However, this particular series is reserved for senior executives. How do most of them learn about it? Direct mail. But not just any direct mail. We carefully design and allocate funds for what I call a "wedding-style" invitation: hand-addressed, in a beautiful envelope, with insert cards that remind of you of the nicest nuptial event you've attended. Expensive? Damn right. But the value of getting a CEO or high-level decision-making executive to come and spend two and a half hours with us is invaluable.

How do we know these printed invitations work?

Because we tested them. We also set up a high-touch registration process where invitees needed to email or call to register. Online registrations are great for the masses, but when that's the only process, the invitees have little to no "skin in the game" and are more likely to cancel or not show up. Especially if the event, live or virtual, is complimentary or at a low enough cost, it's easy to bail on. When we implemented a live, high-touch registration process, however, it was stunning how many C-level participants registered (and registered themselves). You could almost set your watch to it. We'd mail on a certain day, calculate how long it would take the invitation to navigate through their own internal mail system and eventually reach their desk, and almost without fail, the emails would come in or the phone would ring. This was typically an early morning occurrence, between six and seven o'clock, before anyone else was in their office (namely their executive assistant). And when the prospect registered live with someone on our end, there was an implicit bond and tacit agreement made. Cancellations were still common, but no-shows nearly went to zero. These high-level executives had connected with a member of our team on a human-to-human level and didn't want to leave us hanging.

With thousands of executives responding to our direct mail, I am convinced there's a place for it in the marketing mix. Remember, you need an uberaccurate list—interesting, creative, and a clear and relevant offer. If your direct-mail piece cuts through the clutter and you follow up on it, I think it's still a solid bet. Especially now in the deluge of email and General Data Protection Regulation (GDPR) restrictions.

I have dozens of other examples of when direct mail was absolutely the right communication tool to replace a digital message, or in many cases, complement it. Multiple touch points are the key when integrating direct mail with email and phone follow-ups. Early in my career, the norm seemed to be three to four touch points to gain someone's fleeting attention. Then I saw it raised to five to six. Recently I heard it's closer to ten to twelve.

Nobody knows for certain how many touch points it takes to gain a customer's attention. If someone tells you they do, run fast. The point is, direct mail is very relevant for many industries. When you're disciplined enough to know your smallest viable market (Challenge 11) can combine this with reality-based buyer personas (Challenge 20) and you're building lists that matter (Challenge 22), you can then determine if direct mail is a useful arrow in your marketing quiver.

FROM MESS TO SUCCESS:

THE RESPONSIBLE RESURGENCE OF PRINT

- Consider the nature of your product or service, and determine if print marketing:

  - Is irrelevant or detrimental to your brand.

  - Is being deployed because *you* favor it and assume it is what the customer will respond to as well.

  - Is not being deployed because *you* tend to dismiss it and assume the customer will do so as well.

  - Will hit the customer demographic and align to their preferences.

- When using print mediums in your marketing efforts, be certain to heighten your awareness of the environmental impact.

  - Use post-consumer, recycled paper.

  - Sponsor the planting of trees.

  - Offset your footprint with some conservation efforts. Do this because it's the right thing to do, not just for the "currency" with clients. Having said that, it's completely fine to showcase your efforts so your clients know your values and that you're not ignorant, insensitive, or complacent about their impact.

  - Recognize that some parts of the country are much more sensitive than others to paper usage.

CHALLENGE 25

BUILD AND MODEL CONSISTENT BRAND STANDARDS

*Have you developed the wisdom to balance
brand enforcement with localized innovation?*

The power of having consistent brand standards is reinforced to me weekly when I visit Cracker Barrel for lunch on Mondays. Why Mondays, you ask? Well, duh, Monday's lunch special is baked chicken with dressing. For over ten years, this has been the Monday special. (Wednesday's lunch special is chicken pot pie, and it's so good!) Add in some mashed potatoes, a biscuit, and an iced tea, and you've got the best possible work therapy for around $12 an hour. A lot less than $120 an hour for a therapist to basically give me the same outcome—some comfort and peace.

I love Cracker Barrel. And not just for lunch and breakfast (their Country Store is a go-to for the boys' holiday stockings), but also for their consistency. Historically, I traveled nearly every week, and my pot roast and carrots were the same in Columbus, Ohio, as they were in Columbus, Georgia. Exactly the same. So was the service, the prices, the menu, and the atmosphere. I'd call the curated aesthetic somewhat a mix between Sanford and Son's front lawn and Minnie Pearl's kitchen. (I'm guessing a large segment of my readers have zero clue who Sanford or Minnie is, but suffice it to say that both were discs in America's cultural spine in the '70s.)

Cracker Barrel knows what it means to have both brand standards and zero deviation from them. Consistency is key, as is demonstrated in some of the most iconic brands in our history: McDonald's, Crest, Pepsi, The Gap, Palmolive, and hundreds of others. Dr. Pepper is the same in every can you've bought for decades. The cheeseburger tastes the same in every McDonald's restaurant (corporate-owned or franchisee) in every country.

I once spent ten days on a business trip traveling throughout Asia, dining on way too many dumplings, noodle soups, and full-bodied fish. On the eighth day, my Western upbringing left me transfixed as I watched people line up to buy glistening bugs-on-a-stick treats that to my eyes looked more like an entomological display at the Natural History Museum than a treat from the most popular street vendor in Beijing. The nine-inch Chinese skewers had six bugs on them—all perfectly glazed up, spaced out, and impaled down the middle to maximize their culinary and visual appeal. I was more used to a skewer holding melon balls, prosciutto, cherry tomatoes, and mozzarella. Hey, I'm sure many Asian travelers are shocked at the sight of a bloody rare steak or ice in every beverage—different strokes for different folks. But suddenly, I needed some American food—desperately. I wanted a McDonald's cheeseburger.

Admittedly, I probably eat at McDonald's fewer than five times a year, usually for a quick lunch on the run. But while on the final leg of my Asian trip in Japan, my cravings far overwhelmed my need for clean arteries. Alas, David Covey (my leader at the time) and I snuck into a McDonald's and discovered nirvana. Everything was exactly like we'd eaten at home. Couldn't tell the difference. Sure, you could also order some sushi and a few other local delicacies, but the point is that two Americans deep in the bowels of Tokyo fueled up and found a little slice of home to keep us going. And until you've been raised on American comfort food and eaten eight days of full-bodied fish (heads and tails still attached), don't judge me for my culinary cowardice.

Of course, brand standards extend beyond ingredients and menu selections. They impact every client interaction—from your online experience and layout of your stores, to the cash wrap and checkout experience.

Another case in point: I'm a raving fan of Delta Air Lines and have been a loyal flyer for thirty years—I've flown over two million miles with them. I think Delta is a superb example of a global company that integrates brand consistency in every customer experience. I honestly can't tell you their on-time arrival stats, but I continue to experience best-of-class customer service, whether it be in Des Moines, Iowa, Paris, France, or Sydney, Australia. Are there exceptions? Of course. But my consistent experience has been that within the airline industry, Delta's customer service equals or bests most of them. And when you travel almost weekly for three decades, there's great comfort in seeing the iconic "red coat" of the Delta customer-service officer in a far-flung airport.

I think it's actually easier for large, multinational companies to establish (and enforce) brand standards with their associates. If you work at Louis Vuitton or Marriott, here's how you will dress and serve our customers—no exceptions. If you've worked for the Walt Disney Company, you've attended their mandatory "Traditions" orientation class—a required multiday, immersive experience for every "cast member," regardless of your level or whether you work in the parks, a cruise line, a local retail store, or a corporate office. I know this in part because I was one of those cast members back in the '90s.

The bigger struggle with establishing and maintaining brand standards is for the smaller, more entrepreneurial organizations, where independence isn't just encouraged, it's often vital to survival. These companies often include smart, well-intentioned associates who tweak and test new ideas, products, and services faster than they can keep track of. The moment you discover and try to rein in a new field email template or home-produced brochure, the local sales rep has already moved on to another (mastering the art of hiding it from you for as long as possible). I know this because I used to do the same. To avoid a literal marketing mess, empathize with their need to innovate and stay in constant communication with employees around these levels of empowerment. Because absent guard rails, many of them will veer off the road and take your brand with them.

Perhaps call your team together and consider saying something like, "If we want to scale, we need to be aware of creating consistent brand experiences with a culture of innovating and testing new ideas. We need everybody to be hypercognizant of both, and when either of us is being too extreme in either direction. Let's talk about some examples of where we might find ourselves on one side or the other…" Ever heard your CMO offer this invitation, or extended it yourself? Probably not. Brand standards are vital for replicability and creating a flywheel for any organization.

There's both an art and a science to establishing and maintaining brand standards. Some of the most iconic offerings from large restaurant chains, like the Big Mac, were first incubated in the field through a single franchisee and then adopted and scaled through the larger organization. The big idea is, as the leader of marketing, you're the executive, legislative, and judicial branch—you make the rules, interpret the rules, and enforce the rules. But here's the caution: If you're too heavy-handed and suffocate those in the field, they're going to keep doing things off-brand (they just won't tell you and you'll find out too late to influence it). But if you make it safe for them to come to you with ideas—recognizing the lifeblood of innovation comes from those closest to the customer—you can build an unstoppable level of synergy where everyone respects each other's insights, opinions, and responsibilities.

Even larger organizations must find a balance between enforcing consistent brand standards and allowing for some "localized" incubation. When I became the CMO of FranklinCovey, our team inherited a well-established and carefully managed brand. If you're an employee attending a two-day *Speed of Trust* work session at a chemical manufacturer in Los Angeles, it's likely going to be a very similar experience to the one being implemented at a power company in Mississippi or around the world at any organization in Europe or Africa. Brand and reputation are part of our most treasured assets, and the same is likely true for your organization.

One of my first initiatives was to reeducate our global associates about our brand standards, which included fonts, colors, logos, taglines, and anything else in print or digital applications that could be up for local interpretation. Because our hundreds of sales associates are commission-based, they're inclined to be a bit too innovative when creating marketing assets to progress a sale or support a client. Having started my career in sales, I was quite empathic to the practice. But have you ever walked into a Nordstrom and seen a table of locally knitted scarves made by the grandmother of the guy working in the shoe department? Nope, because that's Etsy, not Nordstrom. And collateral printed on a low-resolution laser printer may be great for announcing a child's birthday party, but not FranklinCovey's latest solution. There's a delicate balance between setting brand standards, which are crucial if you want to build and maintain recognizable brand equity, and allowing for and empowering associates to create and innovate based on their proximity to clients and the competition. This is often the lifeblood for breakthrough inventions and business-model disruptions.

To combat rogue laser printers hijacking our global brand, we developed a bold strategy. Our team redesigned every marketing slip sheet (there were hundreds of them) and formatted them to fit custom-size paper. The customized paper, only inventoried in our warehouse, meant that homemade inserts printed on standard 8½- × 11-inch paper wouldn't fit into the custom pocket of the new corporate brochure. In a matter of days, the local design efforts ceased, and a wealth of home printers had to be given other more mundane jobs to do.

The strategy worked so well that we took it a step further. Knowing that listening to the needs of the field is a vital competency, our central marketing team called numerous associates and asked what was still missing—what they needed to accomplish their goals and deliver on their commitments. We analyzed what we'd learned and decided the needs that could be addressed centrally. We planned months in advance of our annual sales conference, attended by every company associate from the CEO to the receptionist. Our team built a custom brand-standards kit that included newly designed double-thick business cards, a set of matching customized note cards with every associate's name and contact information, a company pen, and a small printed booklet that clearly articulated our global brand standards from how to place our logo on a client proposal to approved email signatures. We also included a "Who's Who at HQ" in the booklet so every associate could streamline their efforts when calling on headquarters' staff for support.

The feedback was overwhelmingly positive (not always the vibe at your annual company conference). What we didn't entirely anticipate was the massive pride in the brand that came not just from the elegance of the kit, but from the fact that each one was customized and not a single employee was missed. Everyone, regardless of role, received the branding kit. Associates who'd worked for us for years without a business card, let alone custom note cards, felt a new level of pride. Watching an entry-level associate holding their new (perhaps first) business card is a sight you won't forget. I remember mine, and I bet you remember yours too.

I was reminded of this initiative that took place over eight years ago when I walked past an associate's temporarily abandoned cubical and saw the blue box still sitting on her desk. I'd truly long since forgotten about it. It was one of hundreds of branding projects our team had developed over my tenure. The fact that she still had the kit, and used it, reminded me that marketing isn't a division (Challenge 2) and although everyone owns the brand, marketing has to set and clarify the standards. This mandate is simultaneously balanced with the age-old wisdom that comes from the Japanese sword-fighting art of Kendo: hold the sword like a bird—not so tight as to crush it, but not so loose that it will fly away.

FROM MESS TO SUCCESS:

BUILD AND MODEL CONSISTENT BRAND STANDARDS

- Become hyperaware of what marketing's role should be in your current culture and organization, and in light of new and growing global trends.

  - Determine how successful you've been at maintaining brand standards while allowing for some measure of innovation to take place in the field.

  - Calibrate your point of view, communication style, and level of heavy-handedness with the needs of the business and brand.

  - If possible, create a small team or committee to keep you abreast of the brewing needs and issues in the field that must be addressed before the field creates solutions on their own. As it's often said, "You catch more bees with honey than vinegar."

- Intentionally create a culture where it's safe to talk about frustrations, needs, and "wish list" items that could help further the business. As soon as an "us versus them" culture develops, the metaphorical laser printers come out of storage.

CHALLENGE 26

EVALUATE YOUR
TRADE-SHOW STRATEGY

*Are you caught up in your industry's
legacy of trade-show attendance?*

I'm just going to call it out: Exhibiting at trade shows can be really lame, not to mention physically exhausting, while standing in a booth for three days waiting for the right person you've never met, and didn't know existed, to stop by and have their world blown by your offering.

The odds of this strategy paying dividends are comparable to a single-numbered bet on the roulette wheel in Vegas. Trade shows are a complete waste of time without a strategy.

SIMILAR TO THE OPENING DISCLAIMER IN CHALLENGE 24, I WROTE THIS CHAPTER PRIOR TO THE GLOBAL PANDEMIC BUT VERY MUCH FEEL THE PRINCIPLES I TEACH HERE WILL BECOME RELEVANT AGAIN IN THE NEAR FUTURE.

You have to recognize that trade shows are a massive revenue stream for any conference or association. It's a virtual cycle with big celebrity speakers, a catchy theme, and a named (but not too relevant) band for a one-night concert, all supported by solid breakout sessions. The resulting registrations are the lure for industry vendors to come (some ecstatic and others begrudgingly) and showcase their offerings. Vendors rent convention floor space, and everyone hopes for the best. And on and on, decade after decade.

There are a few exceptions—okay, maybe just one: CES. The Consumer Electronics Show in Las Vegas is a global confab where new technologies are showcased and everyone plans and budgets to one-up everyone else. It's a go-big-or-go-home strategy for every vendor. And if you're not there, you don't exist.

I have great respect for the professional-development and networking value these associations and their conferences provide for their members. I attend several annually. But as far as the trade shows go? Meh! It often feels like they're more for vendors to check up on their competition and sense the market landscape than providing value for conference attendees. Admittedly, that bulging bag of tchotchkes is a bonanza for your kids, but you could save time by visiting Cost Plus World Market instead. That being said, I will come and keynote your association conference and do my best to tip the scales in the other direction. Seriously, I'll crush it for you—just ask my publicist.

But there's a possible upside to exhibiting at a trade show if you plan and execute it well. Regardless of the industry, organizations are confronted with similar trade-show questions: Should we go? Is it worth it? What's the real ROI? What's the impact if we don't show up? Will it hurt our brand? Would we even be missed? Would the funds be better deployed elsewhere? If we do go, how do we ensure it's not just a junket for the eight associates we invite to "work the booth"?

To exhibit or not to exhibit, that is the question.

Plus, there are the thirty additional questions necessary to vet the trade show's value and business return to ensure that attending is a necessity for our company's brand. To move from marketing mess to success, at some point the issue of *brand, brand, brand* needs to convert to *revenue, revenue, revenue!* Remember, you can't deposit brand into the bank and have it fund payroll. Brand may be the means, but it is not the end (and before you wig out and go sideways on me, remember: Challenge 25 is all about brand, so let's move on).

One option, given all the questions above, is to simply bet big on your strategy and then double down just to be sure. Sound crazy? Well, let me share an example of when I did just that.

One year there were four trade-show contenders for us, and we decided to hit all four. Our big bet was the Society for Human Resource Management (SHRM) and we brainstormed our strategy for months. We gathered the entire marketing division and reviewed our previous exhibits to tease out what had worked well and what had flopped. We discussed what we'd seen from our competitors and even exhibits from different industries at different conventions outside of our field. We rigorously debated ideas, mockups, and encouraged even outrageous suggestions as worthy of discussion. Finally, we landed on our *pièce de résistance*.

It would be a showstopper.

We built a massive wall of Amazon Kindles. Over two hundred Kindle Fires filling a twenty-by-twenty-foot-tall wall. Each Kindle was lit and charged by a cord wired through the back. If you're old enough to remember the game show *Concentration* from the '70s, you'll get a sense for how this looked, or *Jeopardy* for you younger folks. Further, all the Kindles were programmed to show the vast collection of FranklinCovey book covers, switching in and out across all of our titles, then on cue coming together to represent one single book. It was quite spectacular. As we were in the midst of construction at the conference, other vendors would come over, speechless, and just stare at both the enormity of the wall and also the technology allowing the synchronized displays. Our former marketing leader and consultant Curtis Morley had built a custom app to program and synchronize these Kindles. The man is a genius! You should connect with Curtis on LinkedIn at: LinkedIn.com/in/curtismorley.

Picture this massive wall of tablets as a giant billboard showing our many iconic, bestselling books. Then, just to take it to the next level, *we gave all the Kindles away!* Every member of the conference had a printed card (designed to look exactly like a Kindle with one of our books on the screen) with a custom ticket that could be scanned to win the real thing. We'd spent seven hours the night before custom wrapping over 10,000 seats in the main auditorium with messaging that read, "Visit FranklinCovey at Booth #3809 to learn more about our solutions and for a chance to win one of 204 Amazon Kindles." Jim Collins, author of *Good to Great* and other well-known business books, was the opening keynote that year, so every seat was full.

After watching thousands of people open their invitations in the main theatre, our team walked back to our booth in the exhibition hall and waited with a mix of anticipation and trepidation. Would anyone show? Would anyone care? We were fairly convinced that if we could "lure" people into our booth, we could use the precious few seconds, while we scanned their potentially winning ticket, to have a short but impactful conversation about adopting our solutions in their organizations.

We were so convinced of our plan we'd actually rehearsed the traffic patterns and conversations in our company gymnasium. We'd planned beyond reason how we thought people would respond and how we could convert potentially thousands of conversations into leads for our sales team.

It was going to be epic.

The keynote ended and the ten of us took our carefully assigned places. Our two electronic scanners were tested and ready to uncover the winners. We had the twenty-foot ladder in place to take Kindles off the wall so passing attendees could see people were actually winning. Our plan (hope) was that over the course of three days, we'd have enough attendees come by and scan their Kindle ticket that we'd at least give away 50 percent of them. Every winner would be asked to post a photo on their own social media, and we'd extend the reach of the campaign beyond the conference. Truly, we'd thought through every detail, both those onsite and those that could sustain momentum postconvention.

It wasn't epic.

It was *beyond* epic.

It was historic.

The keynote ended and the exhibition doors opened. Participants started pouring into the massive hall with nearly all of them descending on the FranklinCovey booth. Think of anxious shoppers as the doors open during a Black Friday sale and you'll get the idea. Within minutes, we had thousands of people crowding around our booth, holding their tickets, trying to figure out if the offer was real and how to win. I clearly remember the crowd with open mouths and eyes agape taking in the sight of hundreds of Kindles perfectly synchronized and flashing FranklinCovey book covers as the first bell rang out and the FranklinCovey team shouted in unison, "WE HAVE A WINNER!" This persisted, nonstop, over three days as our team scanned well over eight thousand tickets.

It was total insanity. So much that the lines to our booth were hundreds deep. I say lines because we had to form two of them that stretched down the main aisle and nearly out the door of the exhibition hall. In theory it was great, but hundreds of people, double file, standing and blocking other booths wasn't our intention, so let's just say we had some unhappy exhibition neighbors (nothing a free Kindle later in the conference couldn't help mitigate). Prize-fueled pandemonium ensued for three solid days as everyone "won" either a Kindle or a consolation prize—a free tuition to become certified as a FranklinCovey facilitator back in their organization.

Little did we know, however, that the conference management team was watching our spectacle from the observation booth above the floor (I didn't even know there was one), and they came down to the exhibition floor and told us the fire marshal was on his way and we needed to break up the lines.

What! The fire marshal? The lines to our booth were *life-threatening*? Are you kidding me? Truth is, the SHRM staff was so overwhelmed with the interest in our booth they didn't know exactly what to do about it (they were in fact great partners in the situation). We did our best to reclaim some semblance of order and move people through the lines as swiftly and smoothly as possible. Not easy, given eight thousand people were having a blast (and some meaningful conversations) as our team handed out company brochures about organizational issues and our solutions. It was magic and surpassed our wildest expectations. For a time-lapse video showing how it all came together, visit ScottJeffreyMiller.com.

So, what would you say—trade-show mess or success? It depends on which lens you view it through and what the objectives of your strategy were. Brand recognition? Bases loaded, top of the ninth, home run wins the game! Revenue invoiced? Pitcher's still on the mound.

Six months after the conference, although we had fewer than ten people redeem their free-certification voucher, we had over 80 percent of the entire conference audience visit our booth and have some level of conversation with our company about their business needs and our solutions. How do we know 80 percent? Because there were ten thousand registrations and we scanned eight thousand Kindle tickets. No doubt, these developed into hundreds of new business opportunities eventually pursued by our field sales force. Success is all how you define it, and when it comes to trade-show ROI, don't delude yourself—it's more difficult to nail down than you think. You, like me, should be vigilant about knowing your trade-show ROI three, six, and twelve months out (depending on the length of your sales cycle), given you're often going to release control of that to the sales force and its dependence upon their CRM documentation. If marketing and sales don't collaborate postcampaign, all the evidence is anecdotal—and that's why most CMOs only have a four-year tenure. As I've relentlessly reinforced in this book, marketing is primarily about business development and revenue. Although a strong, recognizable brand is vital, you can't paper-clip it to the back of your bank-deposit slip.

Did our wall of Kindles build our brand awareness?

Absolutely.

Did it build a pipeline for our sales team to pursue?

Absolutely.

Can I tell you exactly how much revenue was invoiced within twelve months?

Not at all.

But what I *can* tell you is that eight thousand conference attendees were now in possession of not only a FranklinCovey catalog, but a free voucher to teach any of our solutions in that catalog back inside their organization. I would argue that this *name* is in fact the type of *lead* anyone would feel comfortable asking a salesperson to follow up on.

For emphasis, I'm going to repeat this: Connecting ROI to any marketing investment is often greatly dependent on how accurately the sales force ties opportunities and revenue to a particular campaign in your CRM. Was the trade show the procuring cause of the sale, or part of the progression from a C- to B-level opportunity? Was the trade show what initiated a first-level conversation that otherwise wasn't going to happen but which developed over the course of a year, long after the salesperson remembers the trade show's connection? You get the point. It's not completely marketing's responsibility to manage a sales force's CRM documentation. But if you want to get funding for next year's trade show (or some other replacement strategy), you'll be highly invested ensuring the data is as accurate as possible. Of course, this assumes that sales and marketing are in different divisions (which always creates some level of cultural and political tension), but if you want to prove ROI on your marketing initiatives, you must be diligent in understanding what the data presents. Whether it's your team that owns it, or someone else's.

I could share some more successes from trade-show investments, but as I've stated, we learn more from our messes than our successes (and they make much better stories to share over a beer). Here's the potential for trade-show messes: it's far too easy for the spectacle to overshadow your strategy. Trade shows are a tricky marketing investment—invest too little, and you look pitiful; but too much, and you can overwhelm your audience with all show and no substance. To help turn a potential exhibition mess into a success, here are some points to consider before you jump into your next trade show:

- **Be certain the *why* and *what* are fully understood.** Ask yourself why you're attending and what metrics need to be achieved to ensure it was a successful investment.

- **Vet your investment.** Before you commit, pull back and ask how else that investment could be deployed. Is there another way to participate in the same trade show or conference that will further your goals?

- **Know the value of the location.** How important is your location in the exhibition hall? Unless you're renting a massive space, I suggest not very. People will wander and find you on purpose or mostly by accident.

- **Wisely allocate your investment.** How much of your budget is dedicated to your physical structure, marketing collateral, samples, demonstrations, or your "giveaways"? Is that the right balance?

- **Don't do the ordinary.** If you decide to provide every passerby with something tangible (I highly recommend against this), put extraordinary time into designing it. Nobody needs another mint, pen, or squishy. If it's not going to motivate someone to proactively visit your website the

following week or answer your email or call, toss the idea out
and think of something better.

- **Make your value proposition clear.** How prominent is
your value proposition and messaging on your booth?
Can someone tell in three seconds what you offer, and is
it messaged in a way that makes them care, stop, and risk
having a conversation? After all, they're likely just passing
some time before the next session begins (and not looking
to get hijacked). Your messaging needs to be more than your
company name. Miller and Associates means nothing to an
attendee—they don't care that you named your company
after yourself. But a message in huge letters that reads:
"Convert your company to paper-free in thirty days"—now
that's interesting.

- **Know the limitations of "net fishing."** If your strategy is net
fishing and not spear fishing (it must be, or you would never
exhibit), how does this instruct your overall design, offer, and
communication campaign? Scanning three hundred badges
because you had a thirty-second conversation is a total waste
of the five hundred dollars you spent renting the handheld
scanner. A week from now, when attendees are back in their
offices and bombarded by two hundred other trade-show
vendors, why would they remember or pay attention to your
follow-up?

- **Have a follow-up strategy.** Nobody (and I mean *nobody*)
is ever going to call you on their own. I know, you made a
special connection when you smiled, laughed, and even
hugged. Unlike you, they've long forgotten about it by the
time they've boarded the plane for their return flight home
(despite the business card they handed over… one of a
hundred also given out at other booths). The hard truth is
they ain't calling you and they ain't taking your call. It's not
1988 anymore, and your promising lead isn't going to answer
the phone. How many phone calls do you answer from

numbers you don't recognize? And your email? Ninety-eight percent of unsolicited mail is now automatically pushed to clutter or junk (and increasingly, everyone is now wise to your disingenuously personalized message that's been clearly managed by your marketing automation system). So with that depressing diatribe, what are you going to do to break out of the pack and ensure that you can reconnect with the potentially viable opportunities that came from your exhibit? Is it feasible to schedule a time and a day for a follow-up call? Can you hand or offer them something that requires a next step to complete? Could you connect with them on social media or mail something in print to their office that reminds and motivates them of their tacit agreement to engage? You best know your industry and audience. Be pragmatic and creative, because 90 percent of the value that comes from trade shows comes *after* the trade show, not during.

Have I killed your exhibition strategy? I actually hope that's not the case. But a sure way to avoid an exhibit mess is to think carefully through your expectations, strategy, measures, and outcomes. And if you take away only one thing from this challenge, remember: A name is not necessarily a lead and should never be loaded into your CRM with the outcome designed as a task for follow-up by a salesperson. Be very deliberate about setting expectations about what perhaps should continue being nurtured by the marketing team and what is worthy of the sales force's investing time in to pursue on their own.

Further, trade shows often tempt vendors to go big with spectacle instead of crafting a carefully considered strategy (pre, during, and post). And despite the fact that you gave hundreds of pens away at your booth, the reality is no one is going to actually use one to sign a contract of any real significance at the event. The adage when it comes to trade shows is not "Go big or go home"; rather, it's "Go *smart* or go home." Not everyone has the budget for 204 Kindles, but that also means your strategy should never be two fishbowls: one for butterscotch candies and one for collected business cards.

FROM MESS TO SUCCESS:

EVALUATE YOUR TRADE-SHOW STRATEGY

- Brutally confront the likely return you'll see from a trade-show investment by being clear on your goals and calibrating your expectations (including up the corporate ladder).

    - If you think you're going to sign contracts on site, that's delusional.

    - If you think 20 percent of the names you capture will develop into prospects, that's naïve.

- Don't assume anything is free, allowed, or possible at a trade show.

    - Ask endless questions of the conference sponsor to ensure you aren't caught off guard with costs or restrictions.

    - Cost creep at trade shows is guaranteed. Not only do you need to pay to rent the carpet, you may also need to pay to vacuum it.

    - Shipping supplies, especially overnight when you run out on Day One, is a budget buster. Especially when you learn you must pay a union member sixty dollars an hour to deliver the boxes to your booth. Build a budget and plan your project accordingly.

    - Also brace yourself for the union fees when you learn you can't assemble your own booth or bring your own collateral from your car into your space.

- Take a look at the local conferences coming to your city and buy a one-day exhibit pass (most will sell you one). The industry is irrelevant because the learning will be invaluable.

- Walk the floor taking photos and writing notes.

- Evaluate what's working and what's not.

- Gather insights on how to separate yourself from the crowd at your own conference.

- Ask a few dozen exhibitors what their goals for attending are. Gently push on them (after you've disclosed why you're asking) and learn from their strategies or lack thereof.

- Have a plan for how to meaningfully connect with attendees after the trade show.

CHALLENGE 27

NAVIGATE ALL THINGS DIGITAL

What's your process for making digital decisions?

It's impossible for marketers to deeply understand all things digital, let alone become proficient and expert in each of them. The multitude of must-adopt-and-integrate technologies and platforms are dizzying. Just when you've finished implementing your newest CRM (I say newest because sadly, your first CRM is never your last), you need to determine the platform for your website (the first is also rarely your last), and then you're on to selecting your marketing automation service. Next the social media aggregator and distributor—it's never-ending.

If you've got "marketing" in your title, you've got more email in your inbox from different software providers than you have time to read. They all seem to offer the same thing and it's always tempting to believe they're better than what you're currently using. They play on the fear of missing out (FOMO) that we all have, and tap into our insecurities that our tech stack isn't all it can be.

Have you started geofencing? Don't know about geofencing? You're a tech dinosaur in a matter of days or hours now based on the constant push of new tech offerings. How did you ever sell anything to anyone before predictive analytics washed over us all?

Somehow though, we managed.

There's a trove of books, webinars, and podcasts dedicated to every marketing tool, so if you're tempted to earn a PhD equivalent in each, I wish you luck. Amazon is readily willing to enroll you and accept your tuition in eighteen-dollar payments. Instead of trying to conquer them all here, I am choosing instead to offer some sage advice that relates to them all: Start slow and scale up.

These digital tools are now so nuanced and highly specialized that most mid- to large-size organizations are hiring employees focused solely on specific areas. Members of marketing teams own responsibility for narrow tech channels like SEO, social media, marketing automation, email design, etc. Yes, they have to coordinate and collaborate, but the knowledge needed to leverage their individual impact increasingly requires picking one as your specialty.

Like in parenting, just because you *can* doesn't mean you *should*. Does your company really need a Snapchat account when you are selling commercial loans? Are you sure your landscaping business needs a TikTok video? Before jumping in, you need to know where your audience is and which platforms they prefer. Do you really need an enterprise Hootsuite account, or can you get by with a free Buffer account? Which will you pick? Or will you pick any at all?

To help navigate this endless labyrinth of choices, the remainder of this challenge is divided into two big ideas: digital decisions and career decisions.

BIG IDEA NUMBER ONE: DIGITAL DECISIONS

I'm not an expert or a specialist in any particular area of digital marketing (most CMOs aren't), but I do have extensive experience in sourcing, interviewing, identifying selection criteria, securing funding, contracting, implementing and, perhaps embarrassingly, often replacing all of them with the next "right" solution. Consider these recommendations:

Overdeliberate. I've seen countless companies and businesses select the wrong first digital solution, be it their web platform, CRM, marketing automation system—fill in the blank. Similar to your personal life where, for many of us, the most important decision we will ever make is the selection of our spouse or life partner (from which most of your pain and pleasure will flow), your professional marketing life asks the same question: Can you make the *best* decision the first time? I've jokingly heard divorcees refer to their first marriage as either their starter wife or starter husband. Sad or funny, you decide; but for many, it's a very emotional and expensive lesson. The same applies to marketing technologies. Be very careful and deliberate in your selection criteria for all of your digital

MARKETING MESS TO BRAND SUCCESS

decisions. It's another reason to Friend Your Competition (Challenge 15) and not fall victim to the razzle-dazzle features and must-have add-ons that your vendor unveils two weeks after you sign your three-year subscription.

Don't overbuy up front. Resist the discounts, irresistible offers, and shame of not going big out of the gate. Don't become the octomom with your first pregnancy; triplets will sink most parents, let alone a brood of eight. Ease back on the fertility shots, *start small*, and work your way into your digital solutions. Inevitably, I've seen marketers overbuy add-ons that seem "life-or-death vital" during the sales pitch but which, when the rubber meets the road two months in, you can't possibly use because, frankly, you've got to get back to your day job. There's no correlation between the add-on features you buy and the number of hours that suddenly free up in your schedule to leverage them. There is a balance here, of course, as it's your job to make sure the strategy and goals you're working toward are communicated and understood by potential technology vendors wooing your business. But at the same time, recognize that such providers would *love* you to spend your entire day inside their tool—but that ain't gonna happen. So *start small* and don't overbuy. Underbuy and scale later, regardless of the scare tactics your vendor uses to make it financially irresistible (or punitive) not to buy all the additions now. Most, if not all, digital vendors are built on subscription models, and the advantage to load up front is massive… to *them*.

Master and fully implement what you already have. Only add on what you've identified as a "must-have" need, and ignore all the buzz and noise beyond that. Do you have a CRM, and is it fully functional? Don't add an email marketing tool if you're not already collecting data on all of your customer interactions in a CRM. Do you have a viable website that's easy to find and navigate? Are your analytics providing a clear picture, are they informing your design, and are you tracking them religiously? Are your social media marketing tools up and running, and are they giving you the data you need to make better go-forward decisions? You get the idea. Not until your current tech is working to its full potential should you ever look to add on to your stack. It's like putting up outdoor lights outside your basketball court before you've bought the net or own a basketball, and while your children are still in diapers.

Your fear of missing out can cost you more than an early-adopter advantage—it can cost you hundreds of hours of work, massive distraction, significant budget share, and even erode your credibility. Before you start agreeing to phone calls with any number of the vendors who are invariably spamming your work email and your LinkedIn inbox, ask yourself, *Is there anything I am currently invested in that I need to perfect/fix/master before I optimize it?* Too often, marketers find themselves in the mess of overloading their current tech stack before it's fully working for them or, for that matter, even before they know how to work it.

BIG IDEA NUMBER TWO: CAREER DECISIONS

Recognizing that you'll never become an expert at every digital marketing tool, software, integrator, or optimizer; everyone with a marketing career faces a specialist or generalist path, and many don't know which one they're on. I suggest rather than leaving it to chance, you make the choice deliberately.

Let's address your career decisions as they relate to the digital world of marketing. I'd suggest there are two types of marketing professionals: specialists and generalists. This is an idea I gleaned from David Epstein's book *Range,* which is another book recommendation. In my experience, when it comes to marketing, one's not better than the other—but one is likely the right path for you. I'd also say it's possible for specialists to become generalists and generalists to become specialists, but you should know which one best describes you presently, as you're reading this, and figure out whether you landed there deliberately or accidentally.

I worked with a colleague for over twenty years who was a marketing generalist possessing sufficient knowledge of a multitude of marketing strategies—the classic mile-wide, inch-deep professional. This was a fine strategy for her. Then, after my counsel, she moved deliberately into building an expertise in marketing automation, database management, and email design and delivery: three inter-related areas, but far from the dozens of other strategies that remain relevant tools in the overall marketing mix. In less than three years, she can now hold her own with any expert in our industry. Thirty-six months ago, like me, she would have been bluffing her way through a conversation on the same topic. She moved from generalist to specialist in her late forties, and I think this focus has increased her relevance and marketability exponentially—both inside and outside the firm.

Conversely, I've worked with a gentleman in his thirties who is a specialist in social media. Because he's very ambitious, insatiably curious about navigating all things digital, and simultaneously interested in the science of how customers buy and how they refer others to do the same, I would project in ten years he will lead a marketing team responsible for many functions, well beyond social media. He is likely moving from specialist to generalist, putting him on a path that may lead to the C-suite, if he chooses.

Some of you might be thinking that becoming a specialist or generalist is a false choice. Perhaps it is. Without knowing you, I wouldn't prescribe either path or both. However, I do think there's great value in taking some time and reflecting on your future. Is the best strategy to water-ski across many different areas and aggregate as much knowledge as possible along the way? This might be a superb path if you want to become a CMO or marketing equivalent, or if you are planning a side hustle or becoming an entrepreneur and will eventually own all of marketing, albeit on a smaller scale. Alternatively, if you plan on leveraging the security and value that comes with building a longer-term career inside a particular organization, you may well benefit from developing deep expertise in one or more digital areas.

Here are some things to watch out for: I don't know many UX designers with highly specialized digital expertise who will become generalist CMOs. Similarly, generalists can risk fulfilling the adage of becoming a "jack of all trades and master of none." I don't think either strategy or even a deliberate hybrid of both is good or bad; just be intentional with your plans and know the why behind the roles you pursue, the courses you take, the conferences you attend, and the organizations you work with. It may well be that a UX designer becomes a CMO, but they will absolutely need to broaden their portfolio of knowledge to do so.

In case it's not obvious, I'm an unabashed generalist and it seems to have served me well.

FROM MESS TO SUCCESS:

NAVIGATE ALL THINGS DIGITAL

- Remember to *start small.*

  - Don't perpetuate the endless cycle of falling in love and then divorcing because you thought her love of football was real. She never loved football as much as you thought (only the players). Calm down—it was just a metaphor.

  - Enter your digital investments slowly and then scale.

- Know your strategy first, then you can make a brutally honest list of must-haves that you don't buy beyond out of the gate. Contrary to the threats, you can always build and add on features and services. Good grief, it's a digital service, not a car, hotel, or stadium.

- Determine if you're currently a marketing specialist or a marketing generalist.

  - Align your coaching, professional development, and career track to support your specialist or generalist needs.

CHALLENGE 28

DEVELOP YOUR STORYTELLING CRAFT

Who are you casting in the lead role for your stories—you, or the customer?

If you're in a marketing role, there are two people you need to connect to, friend, or follow. I recommend that you download their interviews and read all their books, because the value to your marketing career will be incalculable. What Nancy Duarte and Donald Miller share (other than pure genius and contagiously positive personalities) is their focus on the Hero's Journey. Two key lessons from these experts to help you avoid a marketing mess of your own: simplify your messaging, and cast the customer (not yourself or the organization) as the hero.

Nancy Duarte is the founder of Duarte, a communications-strategy firm based in Northern California. She is the author of numerous books including *slide:olog*y, *Resonate*, *Illuminate*, and most recently, *DataStory*. Her library of writings and tools has transformed my own communication skills, including the decks I build (and perhaps more importantly, the ones I choose not to), the presentations I deliver, the documents I craft, and the stories I tell. Her firm offers a series of open-enrollment courses for individuals looking to transform their communication skills (Duarte.com). I have interviewed Nancy several times for the *On Leadership* podcast, and her knowledge and application of storytelling science, although daunting, can transform your organization's messaging. You'll see her genius illustrated in her own speeches and it will start to stick. Watch her TED talk and begin modeling the process that she calls "the persuasive story pattern." Throughout your story's beginning, middle, and end, you're constantly describing "what is" and "what could be," "what is" and "what could be," "what is" and "what could be," until your hero enters a new bliss, also known as your call to action. Nancy's interview with FranklinCovey's *On Leadership* is a valuable listen—Google "Nancy Duarte On Leadership with Scott Miller."

Donald Miller, the author I referenced back in the Chick-fil-A profile, is also CEO of the Nashville-based communications firm StoryBrand. His *Building a Story Brand* podcast is an absolute must-subscribe. I'm amazed at how many of our *On Leadership* guests listen to his podcast, and nearly all of them are massively influential in their own realms. Google "Donald Miller On Leadership with Scott Miller" to listen to our own podcast conversation. Of Donald's many areas of expertise, pragmatism in messaging is one of his specialties.

In our podcast interview, Donald shared a story about a successful entrepreneur who owned a painting company (as in painting buildings). Donald met him at one of his messaging-and-branding workshops and asked the business owner to pull up his website. After a moment of review, Donald respectfully announced that it looked more like the man owned an Italian restaurant than a commercial painting company. The owner was understandably proud of his heritage and had gotten a bit carried away; he not only needed to choose better images for his site (like photos of his finished homes and businesses), but add clearer language so it was quickly and easily understood what it was he offered. Although tongue in cheek, Donald suggested that a title as painfully obvious as "We Paint Sh#t" would ensure the point wasn't missed.[16] That's what pragmatism in messaging is all about. How much are you overstating what your business does, or sharing things that you may have an emotional attachment to but which aren't germane to the products or services you offer, or more importantly, to what your client needs?

The lesson here? Not all messaging should be told as a story and not all stories should be part of your message. Avoiding a marketing mess around storytelling requires you to differentiate between the two. So what *should* rise to the level of story? The easiest litmus test is to ask *whom* your story is about. In the example above, the painter was eager to tell the story of his heritage. He has every right to be proud of that, but as a marketing story, it's a mess. Marketers who are successful at storytelling cast their customers in the lead role (hero) and not themselves.

How many of us, when writing the copy for our site, emails, direct mail, proposals, etc., are tempted to talk about how much money the organization has invested in research and development? how many clients we have profiled or interviewed? how many times we've implemented this same type of engagement with a client very similar to

---

16   p. 234 Miller, Scott. "Your Customer Is the Hero: Donald Miller," Franklin Covey *On Leadership*. Podcast audio, June 19, 2018. https://resources.franklincovey.com/mkt-olv1/59-donald-miller.

our prospective page viewers? how long we've been in business? how many offices we have? why we founded the business in the first place? what our values are? what our satisfaction or refund policy is? Too much about us and virtually nothing about the customer. Sure, there's value in establishing our credibility, but that can be handled under the "About Us" tab on the website. Don't make it front and center to your storytelling.

I think one of the most challenging aspects to connecting with our clients and customers is building a relationship where *they're* the center of it, not *us*. It's not easy—there seems to be a constant gravitational pull away from them and toward us. And with good reason—we all have egos and are heavily invested in what we create/do/know. It's understandable but not necessarily helpful for our clients when they're struggling to find themselves in our self-absorbed story.

It will come as no surprise if you read my "Acknowledgments" page that I have a partner in writing my *Mess to Success* series. In the publishing industry, they're often called a ghost writer, and they can play different roles. Some authors dictate their books and a ghost writer transcribes it all and fills in the gaps. Others interview the "author" and then set to work for a few hundred hours and write the book for them. Other ghost writers work side by side co-writing every word. None of these apply to how we work together.

I'll use American football as a metaphor to describe my relationship with my ghost writer. I run the ball to the five-yard line (sometimes it's the six-yard line and other times it's the one-yard line). His job is to help me get every chapter from the red zone to the end zone. Sadly, sometimes I pass the football to him and he calls time-out and walks the football back to the twenty. Why? Because he knows that, unless we reset a few yards back, we're going to end up with a field goal instead of a touchdown. His name is Platte Clark and he's a very accomplished Utah-based writer with his own books in print, mostly fiction aimed at the youth market. A master storyteller, he is well steeped in both art and science. His most recent trilogy begins with a book called *Bad Unicorn* (think *Princess Bride* meets *Harry Potter*), and it is one of my oldest son's favorites.

As we discussed the struggle marketers constantly face with focusing on themselves as the hero in their story, he shared with me a superb insight: "Storytelling can feel daunting because it's open-ended. But in truth, there are only four story forms: to win, escape, retrieve, or stop. Maybe the question could be 'What does your customer need to do?' Win (the love of someone via a diamond ring)? Escape (a dull life by going on a cruise)? Retrieve (your dignity through thickened hair)? Stop (erectile disfunction)?"

Your customer is the hero in your story. Not your company, or your mission, or your hard work. Sit down with your team or leaders and discuss the legitimate challenge of not always inserting yourselves into the stories you tell. More likely, you're outright hijacking the story to validate all your hard work and success. Potential clients don't care about the year you were founded, whom you merged with ten years ago, or why your great-grandfather chose the business name (unless you own a pizzeria and the menu doubles as the paper placemat diners can read while they wait). Put yourself in your customer's shoes and think about how they're engaged in winning, escaping from, retrieving, or stopping something relevant to what you offer. That's what they care about. And you'll be surprised at the number of stories that begin to formulate as you simply walk through this exercise.

A frivolous way I build my storytelling skills is with my three young sons. Each night during our bedtime ritual (increasingly ninety minutes... ugh!), after book reading, I turn off the lights and extemporaneously make up a story. They're always a bit nonsensical and meander for four to five minutes until I've depleted all my creativity. Some involve ghosts, castles, princes, firemen, marshmallows, lawn mowers, witches, pinwheels... You get it—often all part of the same story. They make zero sense and they never have a theme (except farting and pooping, which makes them insanely happy). But these top-of-mind fictional stories, which always integrate the boys into the center of them, build my own storytelling abilities and increase my willingness to move outside my comfort zone to better reinforce who the hero really is in their journey. And in case you missed it, the hero is always the three boys, not me. Take the opportunity to make stories up and just run with them. You'll be surprised at just how deep your well of creativity goes.

Avoid a common marketing mess by knowing how to craft a compelling story your customers don't just relate to, but can actually see themselves in. Then instill in yourself and your team the desire and vigilance to not simply cast the client as a supporting character in *your* story but as the hero in *theirs*.

FROM MESS TO SUCCESS:

DEVELOP YOUR
STORYTELLING CRAFT

- Identify your audience, what you want to tell them, and what the moral of your story will be.

  - Write these out *before* you begin crafting your story.

  - If you can't find a moral to your story, it's probably not a story worth telling.

- Identify the driving question your story will answer.

  - Ignore Dale Carnegie's advice to "Tell the audience what you're going to say, say it, then tell them what you've said."

  - Recognize that what drives a story is a question or problem that is satisfactorily answered at the end.

- Accept the fact that every human has stories worth sharing. That includes marketing humans too.

  - Remove any mental roadblocks that suggest you have nothing meaningful to say and give yourself permission to appropriately share your experiences with others.

- Watch Nancy Duarte's TED talk.

  - The more you understand the science of superb storytelling, the easier and eventually more natural it will become for you to craft stories in which you can almost effortlessly integrate your brand with your client as the hero.

- Practice storytelling with your kids, spouse, significant other, or as part of a writing group.

  - Build your narrative muscles by being creative, having fun, and making yourself vulnerable. With enough reps, you might find even yourself on stage at the next Renaissance Festival...

CHALLENGE 29

HONE YOUR WRITING

How are you at reducing your thoughts to writing?

Nearly thirty years ago, I interviewed for a job at the Disney Development Company with the divisional vice president. I remember exactly what I was wearing: brown Cole Haan lace-up shoes, absurdly overstarched khaki pants from Gap, a white button-down Ralph Lauren oxford shirt, a plaid tie, and the requisite blue blazer. How can I possibly remember this? It was the official interview uniform for everyone coming out of college on the East Coast in the early '90s. Quintessential prep. This role was a dream opportunity, as it paid $17.75 an hour (back in 1993, that was like money raining down from heaven), and with a Fortune 500 company to boot. The interview was a must-win for me.

I entered the VP's fairly imposing office after a short and cordial conversation with the VP of human resources (that story in a minute). I sat in front of his desk as he quickly looked over my resume (at twenty-three years old, I shudder to think what I came up with to fill the page). When he was done, he looked up at me and asked a single question that has been forever burned into my memory: "How are you at reducing your thoughts to writing?"

What?

I'd never heard that sentence spoken by anyone in my life. *Reducing my thoughts to writing?* Does he mean can I take dictation? Do I know shorthand? I wanted to ask him to rephrase the question, but fortunately, I quickly ruled that out (and when I say quickly, I mean like in a tenth of a second). I replied with unrivaled bravado, "Excellent actually, thanks for asking—this is one of my true talents."

Let's revisit the conversation, if you could even call it that. I didn't understand any part of his question, but my answer was a winner. Pathological? Perhaps. But remember, this interview was a must-win for me—$17.75 an hour could buy a lot of khakis. The VP looked at me, smiled politely, and said it was nice meeting me, and I was excused from his office. Later that afternoon, I got the call that I'd been hired.

Boomshakalaka!

The thought of reducing my thoughts to writing never entered my mind again... until three days later when I began work Monday morning.

I'll return to the coming mess in a moment, because I have to segue and share the details of the interview with the VP of human resources.

This lady was composed and professional. I was young, but not so young that I failed to understand that she'd be analyzing me every minute of our conversation; Disney is quite adept at profiling its new hires. We spent about twenty minutes together. She talked about the projects I might be assigned to, and asked about my education and previous work experience (did washing dishes, waiting on tables, mowing lawns, and waxing cars even count?) Then came the penultimate question. She asked me with a straight face: "What song best represents who you are as a person?"

What?

Did she really just ask me what song best represents who I am as a person? Is she going to ask me about my preferred superhero alter ego next?

One look at her expression told me she wasn't kidding. Without any hesitation I pulled the best "you should hire me" song completely out of my ass: "Gloria Estefan's, 'Get on Your Feet, Get Up and Make It Happen.' "

Winner-winner chicken dinner Scott Miller!

I stayed at Disney for nearly four years. Now back to my self-created marketing mess:

I reported to work the following week to deliver on my natural writing "talent." Part of my job was to help craft press releases, invitations to marketing events, correspondence with corporate partners, slide decks and presentations, business plans, and a whole bevy of "Disney-quality" private and public communications. It's no exaggeration to report I had my college public relations textbook open (on my lap, under my cubicle desk) for four solid years trying to compose anything that remotely met Disney standards. A complete, unmitigated mess is the only valid description of my writing capabilities. At every turn, my documents were returned and marked up worse than my high school British lit essays. It was embarrassing and emasculating, and I spent hundreds of sleepless nights convinced I was going to be exposed and terminated. At one point it became so untenable that my leader at the time looked at me over lunch and said (this is so viscerally burned into my memory that I can recall it word for word thirty years later), "Scott, you don't get it. I need someone who gets it."

The fact is, I didn't get it. I was wholly unqualified for the job, but those four years at Disney taught me that my writing deficits could not continue if I was going to pursue a career in any role, in any organization. Disney gave me a wonderful gift of realization and self-awareness, and it changed the trajectory of my marketing career.

Okay, thanks for allowing me to indulge in this setup. Now let's get serious about your writing. This is a competency everyone in a marketing career (or any professional career for that matter) needs to develop and master. There is a national crisis of underwhelming writers inside organizations. Okay, maybe a tad hyperbolic, but most people can't write. And neither could I when I came to work that first day at Disney (or for that matter, the last day), even after a litany of public relations and writing classes. As it turned out, the ability to reduce your thoughts to writing simply means: *Can you write*? Can you take what's in your head and convert it into a cogent and professional email, document, letter, or any type of written correspondence that might need to inform or persuade someone? And can you do it with brevity, eloquence, logical transitions, proper grammar, and consistency in style?

I don't care what your professional role is: you must learn to write. And write well. And there's only one way to do it. Just like dating, it's about VOLUME. VOLUME. VOLUME. Nobody I've ever met came out of college ready to write professionally (sorry, English majors). It's a skill that builds only with reps in the real world. Like hundreds and thousands of them. It's about you trying over and over again to perfect your style so it matches that of your organization. There are so many potential marketing messes tied to the inability to write that I can't overstate the importance of paying the price to build your writing skills. Here are some thoughts to consider that worked for me. (You may think I need a dose of my own medicine, but it's my ~~party~~ book and I'll ~~cry~~ write what I want to.)

- **Find a mentor who can write well.** Ask them to take you under their wing and teach you some of their wisdom and best practices. This may seem unrealistic, but if you can find a seasoned associate, it can prove invaluable. I've always found that when people have an expertise and someone desires to learn from them, as long as that person is paying the price to improve, the mentor's level of investment is nearly endless.

- **Select a skilled writer on your team or one who sits nearby and can proof your correspondence for a set period of time.** This may feel suffocating at first, but it will pay off in the long run. The more you see and make edits suggested by others, the quicker you'll adopt them into your style. This will not happen in two weeks—it will take months and hundreds of marked-up emails and memos for your writing to improve.

- **Consider shopping your work around to a variety of people so you can get different perspectives.** Whatever you do, thank them for their feedback and don't become defensive. For every important document I craft, I always have multiple people proof it before sending. This has saved me countless occasions of embarrassment and materially improved my grammar, punctuation, spelling, transitions, etc.

- **Ask some of the more seasoned writers in your organization to share with you several samples of their own writing so you can keep them handy for reference.** Not to copy, but to benchmark against.

- **Recognize that writing is like cooking.** Baking is very different from grilling, and writing web, social, and email copy is vastly different from writing proposals, handbooks, and legal documents. Learning the subtle differences between internal and client/public-facing work is also imperative and likely requires very different word choices and style differences.

- **Read.** Turn off the television and radio and try binging on a book over the weekend instead of Netflix. You might also consider taking a podcast sabbatical. No other medium is more effective at building your vocabulary than the printed word. Simply put, reading builds your word bank. I once read that renowned rapper and songwriter Eminem (Marshall Mathers) memorized significant parts of the dictionary to increase his vocabulary so extemporaneous rapping and songwriting would be easier for him. Like him or not, a study found he integrated over eight thousand words in his lyrics (compared to the Spice Girls who fell just short of fifteen hundred words).[17] Take that, fans of late '90s British pop!

- **Improve your transitions.** Sentences need to flow smoothly from one to another. Practice writing prose with natural transitions, not stilted sentences.

- **Remember that brevity and clarity are paramount.** Many of us (me) write how we talk, and that can be both entertaining and exhausting. Shorter is always better.

- **Structure your documents.** Do you understand the value of structure—or for that matter, can you draw upon different templates for your documents—or does the information just flow from your brain spontaneously? Paragraphs need to build and connect smoothly. There's a science to crafting your documents, and only after you've learned the rules can you consciously break them.

- **Explore the available resources.** Online and live workshops can improve your writing skills. Invest the time, as the return will be palpable in both your contribution and brand.

---

17   Jewalikar, Varun, and Verma, Nishant (2015) "The Largest Vocabulary in Music," *Musixmatch*, June. Available from: http://lab.musixmatch.com/largest_vocabulary/.

The sad truth is, I've never met a person who said they couldn't write. And those who announce they *can* typically *can't*. You'll tell me you can't spell or "can't do math" with little hesitation, but few of us acknowledge our writing limitations. In the words of Kurt Vonnegut: "We have to continually be jumping off cliffs and developing our wings on the way down." So buy some red pens, hand them out to your selected colleagues, and announce this is the year you're going to take the leap and transform your writing—with their help. With enough reps and willingness to be coached, you too can soon describe your remarkable talent for reducing your thoughts to writing. And in your case, it will be the truth!

FROM MESS TO SUCCESS:

HONE YOUR WRITING

- Consider this quote by Ernest Hemingway: "We are all apprentices in a craft where no one ever becomes a master."[18] Confront your own reality: how would others describe your writing? Family members don't count.

- Inventory your writing strengths and weaknesses.

  - Are you too verbose?

  - Can you weave thoughts seamlessly together with smooth transitions?

  - Is your writing style right for your company's brand and industry?

  - Appropriately leverage your strengths and create a plan for addressing your weaknesses (there are hundreds of writing resources available online).

- Make sure you own *The Elements of Style* by Strunk and White. It has been the gold standard for the correct use of grammar and other writing topics for over fifty years. Read it once and then keep it within arm's reach.

- Read more and dissect what you admire.

  - Expand your interaction with the written word by reading more novels, magazine articles, professional blogs, biographies and memoirs, etc.

  - Evaluate the themes, voices, turns of phrase, dramatic structure, or other elements that make a piece resonate with you.

  - Look to model that in your own writing, as applicable.

---

18   p. 245 Hemingway, Ernest. *The Wild Years*. New York: Dell Publishing, 1967.

- Create a grid that captures all the types of writing you do: emails, advertising copy, contracts, web content, marketing slicks, etc.

  - Next to each type, indicate the predominant style required: expository (explaining a concept), descriptive (using words to paint a picture of a person, place, or thing), persuasive (convincing someone to do or believe something), and narrative (communicating a story that includes characters, settings, and conflict).

  - Go online and study the best techniques for the required style types and incorporate them into your writing.

CHALLENGE 30

SET AND CHALLENGE YOUR QUALITY STANDARDS

Does everyone in your organization define quality the same way?

About fifteen years ago, I was serving as the managing director of a forty-person team spread throughout fifteen states. The core support team worked with me in the central office—about fifteen of us functioning like a closely knit family (with all the good and bad that comes with "family"). And I was the dad, offering my advice as most dads do—with all the dreams, insecurities, jealousies, lapses in judgment, expertise, and the slew of messes that come with being a "parent." (Which is to say you should be nicer to your familial and organizational parents, because both jobs are fairly unrewarding and thankless.)

We had a small copy room in the office with everyone's mailbox, the printer, all the office supplies, and the holy grail of business in 2003: the fax machine. Business life, for about twenty years, revolved around faxing. Scanning documents via email and DocuSign wasn't a thing yet, and if you wanted a signed contract in by quarter's end, you spent a lot of time huddled around the fax machine, staring, waiting, watching, praying. I can remember loading a roll of specialized fax paper in the machine long before you could just insert standard copy paper in the tray. I also walked four miles uphill to school... both ways... in the snow...

One day I was in the copy room and a colleague was preparing to send a fax. He was completing the vital fax cover sheet, as most offices shared a fax machine among divisions or large teams, and faxes needed to be routed to the correct recipient. I'm not sure why, but I leaned over his shoulder to see what he was faxing. (Truth be told, I know exactly why... I was a micromanaging, tyrannical leader and a busybody as well—hey, it may be the final chapter, but there's still room for more of my messes.) The associate was furiously crossing something out with a pen, and I asked what he was doing. He responded that he was faxing some details about a client event to one of our internal consultants and had spelled her name wrong on the cover sheet. I was a bit horrified that he was scratching out the name with all the delicacy of a spasmodic gopher.

I took a deep breath and suggested he use a new cover sheet.

I will never forget his response: "It's okay, it's just Janet."

It's just Janet?

I took the moment to teach a lesson about quality standards. There's no such thing as "just Janet." Not internally, not externally. Not even in purgatory. Everyone deserves a clean fax sheet literally and metaphorically.

I reinforced how important it was to treat Janet with respect and not send a cover sheet full of corrections and scratchings, but he persisted, saying I was obsessing over small details. I was, which is exactly the point of this chapter.

"It's just a fax, Scott, relax," he said.

I reinforced that this was not the standard for our brand as he dug in further. Then I lowered the velvet hammer on him: Was this acceptable as the standard for *his* brand? He blinked several times as he thought about it, and I knew I'd won the battle (and probably the war). The war of course being our and *his* brand.

That's right—whatever quality standards you find acceptable for the organization are also the quality standards associated with *your* brand. Why? Because where you set the bar for quality standards will have a systemic effect across everything you do. Whether this ends up being a mess or success is completely up to you.

I once attended an internal product launch event with fifty senior salespeople. During the afternoon break, we gathered in the hallway to see what snack was being offered. It's a time-honored tradition that in any day-long session, the afternoon snack is paramount to raise the energy levels after a heavy lunch and sustain the audience for the remaining few hours. We reached the twelve-foot table and found ourselves staring at a brown grocery-store paper bag, turned on its side and torn open in the middle, exposing a lump of room-temperature soft pretzels accompanied by a small bottle of mustard with the plastic safety wrap still sealed around the top. No plates. No napkins. No utensils. No nothing. My six-year-old son could have presented the soft pretzels with more quality and care and would have at least delighted in gnawing the plastic off the mustard top.

What's the quality issue you ask? If this was the amount of thought they put into their break, imagine how little they put into their client service. Minimally, the soft pretzels should have been warmed up, put on a platter, the mustard poured into ramekins—anything to show they gave a crap about their audience. In case you think I'm fixated on pretzels, I don't even like pretzels (hard or soft). But I know how to treat people respectfully and with a high quality standard. And it wouldn't have cost anything to put a couple of moments of extra care into the presentation.

My nearly four years working for the Disney Development Company, a subsidiary of The Walt Disney Company, taught me volumes about quality. That hundred-dollar-plus, one-day park pass you just bought... you'd be surprised how little of that is profit, because they put so much into the quality of the experience. The profit is actually found in the soda, balloons, turkey leg, cotton candy, and plush toy you exit with. Disney is not cheap in cost or quality. As a cast member, I had an inside look into the vast investments they made in employee training, park security, obsessive safety precautions, developing new and innovative rides and experiences, and licensing content outside of their own creation to ensure the customer's experience is always top-notch. The maintenance and improvement costs invested in rides, floats, and entertainment venues is nonstop. Disney is a superb model for quality, hence the establishment of The Disney Institute so that teams from outside organizations can learn "The Disney Way."

Of the many parts of FranklinCovey I appreciate, I admire our commitment to quality. It shows up in the diligence of our research, the design of our solutions, the production of our tools and videos, the facilitation skills of our consultants, and every process in between that our clients don't see.

Included in this standard is the quality of our marketing and communication efforts. As a global company, the volume of information we distribute is dizzying. With offices in nearly a hundred countries, the coordination and updating of information is nonstop. We treat all of our "Janets" exactly the same—as if they're the only one and their experience with us matters. When something is ready to be "public-facing," we have a rigorous system of checks. Every significant piece of correspondence must pass a three-person review process, not including those who helped produce it. And the three people must be from a carefully selected group of six pre-approved associates deemed editorially qualified by the CMO. Then, if there are any disputes, our head writer makes the call and we support their final decision. You'd be surprised how often they have to cast the deciding vote in a company with very competent authors, editors, and book experts. This seemingly absurd process raises the level of everyone's work and eliminated all but two printed errors during my seven years as CMO.

Consider the story of Ed and Steve Sabol, the father-and-son team behind the hugely successful NFL films. When others were looking to simply capture the game on video, Ed wanted to show football in the same way Hollywood crafts movies. In a CBS News interview, Steve remarked about his father's decision to shoot on film rather than the much less expensive videotape: "If *Lord of the Rings* had been shot on videotape, it wouldn't have the same sense of wonder, of majesty, of magic about it. We're historians, we're storytellers, we're mythmakers. We'll always stay on film."

Ed Sabol created four quality rules their fledgling company would follow:

Rule 1: Shoot film and only film, even though it costs much more than videotape.

Rule 2: Have at least one camera shoot the action entirely in slow motion, even though it consumes more film and costs more money. (As a result, it's often said they turned brutality into ballet.)

Rule 3: Don't ignore the sound.

Rule 4: Use the voice of God to narrate the films.

As Ed said, "You remember the quality long after you forget the price. Of anything. And the quality always comes first."[19]

---

19   Leung, Rebecca (2004) "Father-Son Team Establishes Gold Standard for Sports Photography," *CBS*

A fateful twist in the story of the young man in the copy room scratching across the fax cover sheet: He went on to develop a fantastic career, including coaching others on their own quality standards. He eventually left, earned his MBA, and pursued some fantastic career opportunities. He and his wife had three boys, and tragically, while living in Wyoming on a job assignment, he was killed by a drunk driver one morning as he was riding his bike to work.

Matt Harker, your legacy lives on in the lives of countless people and you will never be forgotten. I dedicate *Marketing Mess to Brand Success* to you. And by the way, I'm sure our mutual friend and colleague Janet forgives you—I just hope you forgive me for using your fax story as the main thrust of this challenge. You should know that your wife Stacy is doing you proud raising your sons alone. They were all over for dinner recently and I just marveled at what fine gentlemen they're becoming. You're missed, Matt. You were one of the good ones!

So don't scratch through your faxes. Be humble enough to ask others to proof your work, and accept their advice. Don't drive after you've been drinking. Be kinder to your parents and leaders. And whatever you do, put the soft pretzels in the microwave and hit "fifteen seconds." Life is too short and precious to be minimized by anything less than the highest-quality standards—in every area of life and work.

News, 26 Jan. Available from: https://www.cbsnews.com/news/nfl-films-inc-26-01-2004.

FROM MESS TO SUCCESS:

SET AND CHALLENGE YOUR QUALITY STANDARDS

- Recognize that, absent facts, people make stuff up. This timeless public relations principle is relevant to your quality standards in marketing. Absent you setting a high standard, others will set their own (and often lower than that preferred by you and your organization).

  - Take the time to visually demonstrate your own quality expectations.

  - Remember that people are invigorated by clarity and fatigued by confusion.

  - Is everyone on the team crystal clear on what's acceptable and not? If there's any confusion, you own it.

- There's a reason every Denny's kitchen has high-gloss, full-color photos of every menu option hung up for the cooks to see. It helps ensure as it's plated up to the window that it looks (and hopefully tastes) just like the menu promised. What's your equivalent?

- Don't assume *your* quality is the standard. Be aware that others may in fact have a higher (or different) view and theirs may be best adopted.

  - Are your own expectations realistic? replicable? sustainable?

  - Be humble enough to change your mind and raise your own standard to the level of someone else's if that's the case.

CONCLUSION

Many of the reviewers who edited this manuscript prior to publication gave me similar feedback: "This is as much a leadership book as it a marketing book."

I suspect that's true, given my entire thirty-year career has been dedicated to leadership development, and the majority of what I read deals with business and life leadership. My hope is that you benefited from some principles that have governed my career, most of which has been in sales and marketing. I didn't try to chase every trend, identify every emerging technology, or give you a "how to" guide on marketing techniques taught in college. To the contrary, I tried to share valuable lessons, many learned from my messes, so that you can not only avoid living them yourself, but contemplate how you can leverage them to your own success.

"Own your mess" has become a mantra I repeat at nearly every speech I give. I've decided to continue to share my messes regardless of my next career milestones, because truth be told, everyone already knows them. And the same is true for you. Regardless of where you are in your career, you've got a slew of messes in your past, and soberingly, more to come. But here's the key: The more you own and teach from them, the safer you make it for others to own theirs.

Imagine a work culture where the leader consistently gathers their team around and teases out the lessons learned and principles unearthed from their recent messes—inconsequential messes and consequential messes alike. This takes a level of vulnerability most leaders lack because they've been taught to stand tall, be confident, lead from knowledge and experience, and show unwavering faith in their charted course. Some of this is helpful. Most of it isn't.

People want to relate to their leaders—to learn from them and confide in them about their own fears and passions; to share what excites them and admit what bores them; to reveal what confuses them and confide what intimidates them. By owning your messes and making them a tool for learning, you become the leader your team and colleagues want to sit down with and authentically share not only their messes, but their successes too. If you combine the lessons from this book with those in *Management Mess to Leadership Success*, you'll have a significant edge over someone else fumbling around in their own unacknowledged messes.

I intentionally chose to author more of a career guide than a book on marketing fundamentals. I now invite you, if you see someone struggling in their own marketing career, or in any career for that matter, to consider gifting them a copy. Not to benefit me, but them! Saving people from themselves is the hallmark of my own career, and I've been saved from *myself* many times by others who cared about me and my brand. So please accept the wisdom found in both my messes and successes and add them to own to your experiential tableau as a leader, colleague, companion, spouse, and friend.

ACKNOWLEDGMENTS

When I first wrote *Management Mess to Leadership Success*, I hoped it would be well received (given I'd never written under my name publicly, other than in a few dozen LinkedIn articles). BAM—the book became a multiweek bestseller and won BookPal's OWL (Outstanding Works of Literature) award in the leadership category. It ignited in me a passion to share more of my messes (don't worry... I have a vast supply after a three-decade career), and so next came *Marketing Mess to Brand Success*.

Where to start in sharing the credit:

Chris McKenny, the founder and publisher at Mango Publishing in Coral Gables, who lowers my blood pressure every time I talk with him. He's my alter ego in every aspect, and that's a great thing to have in a publisher as you're navigating the constantly changing landscape of this world. The team he's built at Mango has become a powerhouse in the publishing world; likely why in a short time, Mango has been recognized as the fastest-growing independent publisher in the nation.

MJ Fievre, my Mango editor and sounding board. MJ is an accomplished author, published in many languages, and provides me with invaluable guidance when something I've written just doesn't come to life on the page like it does in my head. One part muse, one part literary therapist, one part school principal. Together they are the ideal combination for my writing style.

The many friends and colleagues who generously gave of their time to read the book and offer hundreds of edits, including suggestions about what they liked and hated. This group of loyalists includes Sue Dathe-Douglass, Rafat Fields, Valerie and Barry Boone, Scott Bishop, Stan Thibeault, Marianne Phillips, Michael Miller, Mary Crafts, Jon Lofgren, Deb Lund, Paul Walker, Jennifer Stenlake, Lauri Hawkins, and others I am sure I've missed. Thank you all for your selfless gift of time and support.

Stephanie Miller, my wife, confidant, critic, and best friend, read every word in the book, multiple times. With absolutely no marketing background, she was the perfect sounding board to tell me when something was nonsensical (both in my life and in this book).

Drew Young, a FranklinCovey associate who originally suggested the idea for a *Mess to Success* series. Authors, editors, and publisher aside, it was Drew's genius that set up the series. So, if you hate them, blame Drew.

Laney Hawes and Reid Later, thank you both for the superb copyediting, legal permissions, and other vital parts of publishing nobody ever sees.

Platte Clark, who serves as the architect for the *Mess to Success* series and is my trusted writing partner. Platte is a genius. His patience, humor, perseverance and, most of all, tolerance for my extemporaneous, sometimes indecipherable, and often incoherent writing style is key to finishing these manuscripts that hopefully add value to each reader.

I appreciate you Platte.

Scott Jeffrey Miller

Capping a 25-year career where he served as chief marketing officer and executive vice president, Scott Miller currently serves as FranklinCovey's senior advisor on thought leadership, leading the strategy, development, and publication of the firm's bestselling books and thought leadership.

Miller hosts the FranklinCovey-sponsored *On Leadership with Scott Miller*, the world's largest and fastest-growing leadership podcast, reaching more than six million people weekly. Miller also authors a leadership column for Inc.com and *Utah Business*, and hosted the weekly iHeart Radio show *Great Life, Great Career*.

Miller is the author of the multivolume *Mess to Success* series, including *Management Mess to Leadership Success: 30 Challenges to Become the Leader You Would Follow* (2019), *Marketing Mess to Brand Success* (May 2021), and *Job Mess to Career Success* (January 2022). He is the coauthor of the *Wall Street Journal* bestseller *Everyone Deserves a Great Manager: The 6 Critical Practices for Leading a Team*, and the author of *Master Mentors: 30 Transformative Insights From Our Greatest Minds* (September 2021), which features insights from his interviews with the leading thinkers of our time, including Seth Godin, Susan Cain, Stephanie McMahon, General Stanley McChrystal, and many others.

In addition to supporting FranklinCovey's global thought leadership efforts, Miller developed the ignite your genius™ coaching series to help leaders take their careers from accidental to deliberate. He also hosts FranklinCovey's Bookclub.com series with world-renowned authors, launching in April 2021.

Prior to his roles as chief marketing officer and executive vice president of business development, Miller served as general manager and client partner in FranklinCovey's Chicago and U.K offices. As a highly sought-after speaker and podcast guest, he has presented to hundreds of audiences across dozens of industries and loves to share his unique journey as an unfiltered leader thriving in today's highly filtered corporate culture.

Miller began his professional career in 1992 with the Disney Development Company (the real estate development division of The Walt Disney Company) as a founding member of the development team that designed the town of Celebration, Florida.

He and his wife live in Salt Lake City, Utah, with their three sons.

SJM

Scott Jeffrey Miller

TO SPEAK AT YOUR EVENT

Are you planning an event for your organization? Schedule Scott Miller to deliver a high-energy and engaging keynote speach, tailor-made for todays marketing leaders at events including:

- **Association and Industry Conferences**
- **Sales and Marketing Conferences**
- **Executive and Board Retreats**
- **Annual Meetings**
- **Company Functions**
- **Onsite Consulting**
- **Client Experiences and Engagements**

Scott's professional roles have evolved as he became a multi-bestselling author, radio and podcast host, leadership coach, columnist, and global keynote speaker.

Scott currently serves as the Special Advisor on Thought Leadership for the FranklinCovey Company and is the host of their weekly podcast series, *On Leadership with Scott Miller*. Scott also hosts FranklinCovey's monthly bookclub on Bookclub.com debuting in April, 2021. Additionally, Scott is the prolific author of numerous books, writes a column for *Inc. Magazine*, and keynotes for clients around the world.

To schedule Scott Miller today,

call: **1-801-201-7445** or visit: **scottjeffreymiller.com**

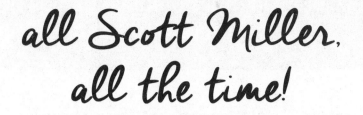

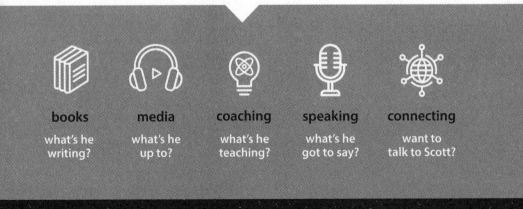